LOOKING FOR FLYBOYS

©2014 Tom Messenger

Published by Hellgate Press

(An imprint of L&R Publishing, LLC)

Hellgate Press
PO Box 3531
Ashland, OR 97520
email: info@hellgatepress.com

Editor: Harley B. Patrick
Cover Design: L. Redding
Cover Photo: Courtesy of Robert Vickery

Cataloging In Publication Data is available from the publisher upon request.

Printed and bound in the United States of America
First edition 10 9 8 7 6 5 4 3 2 1

To all the flight crews, maintenance teams, allied shops, and command personnel for their perseverance during the Vietnam War. Their skills kept the CH-47 Chinook in the air performing its duties for all the infantry units in the field. It is my hope that this book sheds some light on our sacrifices.

TABLE OF CONTENTS

LOOKING FOR FLYBOYS

TOM MESSENGER

HELLGATE PRESS   ASHLAND, OREGON

I

Everyone Has A Number

PEOPLE OFTEN ASK ME, "WHAT MADE YOU JOIN THE ARMY?" Or sometimes, "What made you join the Army Air Corps?" Often it's, "What were you thinking?" And even, "What in God's name were you thinking?"

It all began as I rode to work on the Rock Island train to Chicago. As I looked over the many faces, I saw the same blank stare and I thought to myself, *That's me in ten to fifteen years.* They were staring across the coach, thinking about their mortgages, their kid's dental bills and tuition, and yes, their wives.

I tried talking to these guys. All they could talk about was their kids, their wives, and sports. Every once in a while a good-looking lady would walk down the aisle and grab their attention. They would make a remark, a face, or a gesture. They were harmless, and every one of them insisted they were an expert on sex. These men vowed they were happy, but their faces betrayed them. I wondered if these guys had any adventure in their lives.

I just knew there had to be more. Everyone was following the same pattern and I was about to do the same. It looked like high school, college, job, marriage, kids, mortgage, bills, bills, etc. Was this the order God wanted? It seemed most of the time life unfolded this way. Why couldn't I find adventure and have sex with a girl anytime I wanted, and not have a mortgage, kids, and bills (except a car payment for a 1962 Corvette)? It didn't get any better than that.

I left the LaSalle Street station and walked east on Jackson. I heard a loud clapping noise coming from the east. I looked up and saw three cool Army helicopters. I identified them as Bell UH-1s, otherwise called "Huey's." I was awestruck by what I saw. This was my epiphany. I knew it same as God made little green apples. I had to get on those helicopters, that day, that minute, that second. It wasn't about the other guys on the train. They had chosen their path; it was my turn to pick a path. I noticed I had a little spring in my step, a little swagger, and yes, a little bit of cockiness. I just had to find a way to get on those choppers.

I walked into the nearest Army Recruiting Center and asked, "Where do you keep the helicopters?"

The recruiter looked at me with a big smile on his face and said, "We usually keep them at a fort or Army airfield." Vietnam had been raging now for about five years and the Army was not too well thought of. My draft number was pretty low so I had to make a move. I was thinking if I signed on for an extra year I could get the job I wanted in aviation. I had a lot of questions to ask the recruiter, and he answered them all.

Recruiters are the Army's salesmen. If they need pilots, they go after people for pilot slots; mechanics, artillery, whatever it takes. In the old days they could embellish quite a bit. Remember, there are no French chefs in the Army, just cooks who are of French descent. I signed up for three years so I could get aviation mechanics. That could lead to a crew status like crew chief or flight engineer.

I signed up to leave on Jan 6, 1970. I went home to tell my parents. My mother was beside herself and beside her was my father, who was proud but concerned. At first I thought he took the news rather well, but he kept insisting I try pro baseball again. We both knew whenever a pitcher would throw a breaking ball my knees would buckle. I was the third oldest of nine kids. A year ago they had moved me from the upstairs bedroom to the back porch bedroom. They were slowly edging me out.

2

LIFE AS I KNEW IT WAS
ABOUT TO CHANGE

M Y FATHER DROVE ME DOWN TO THE INDUCTION CENTER on Van Buren St. in Chicago. He was offering tidbits of information about the Army and how to survive Basic Training and AIT (Advanced Individual Training). The last thing he said was, "Try to keep that smart mouth of yours shut." As I got out of the car he tried to say more but the words never came out. He hugged me and I walked into the building. I knew what he was thinking: He had gone to war so I wouldn't have to, but the plan hadn't worked out. America has its wars. We are a fighting nation, and I sometimes think we love it. About a hundred of us took the oath that day and boarded a bus bound for Ft. Campbell, Kentucky.

A sick, queasy feeling came over me, and it reminded me of the first time I had gone to church summer camp. That was for two weeks; this was for three years. As I looked around the bus, I saw guys from all over the Midwest. They all had the same look of bewilderment. Was this going to be a great experience, or was this next eight weeks going to be a laborious and torturous time in our lives? I will tell you this: If you have the proper frame of mind, you can get through times of uncertainty like this.

The bus pulled into the Ft. Campbell Welcoming Center. What a misnomer this was. Two soldiers got on the bus. Their uniforms were neatly pressed and tailor-made for their bodies. They had these round, brown hats on, like Smokey the Bear wears.

All of a sudden they started yelling at the top of their lungs. They had the most irritating voices I'd ever heard. They were speaking a new lingo I had never heard before: "Get into formation, form four ranks, dress right dress, right face (*this is my right face*), left face, (*yes I have a left side of my face*), come to attention, at ease (*nobody was at ease*)." This was a gaggle of men milling around, trying to satisfy the needs of two crazed Drill Sergeants.

Drill Sergeants, by the way, are not your friends; they are not kind, not understanding, not compassionate, not forgiving, not your big brother, not your advisor, and most of all, not human. They are loud, commanding, sadistic, short-tempered, and intolerant of rule-breaking and infractions. In all fairness, their main objective is to give you an even chance on the field of battle. It's all about acting and reacting, and most of that is mental. They have to break you down so they can build you up. The Army has been doing this for years and it works. Just don't take it personally.

The Drill Sergeants addressed us as trainees, maggots, pieces of dung or whatever else came into their minds. They started inspecting the ranks and taking a good look at us, stopping at every fourth soldier and asking, "Where are you from?" The men would answer, "Iowa," "Wisconsin," "Michigan"; they were from all over. One of them instructed us to call him "Drill Sergeant"; his title was that important. He stopped in front of me and there was an awkward moment of silence between us, and I couldn't stand it anymore.

I blurted out, "How's it going, Sarge? Where do you keep the helicopters around here?" As I waited for an answer I saw his face turn red. His nostrils flared and his eyes bugged out so much I could see the little capillaries in the whites of his eyes. Then it came: Mount St. Helens started to erupt. That irritating voice was once again booming, this time three inches from my left ear. He commanded I get into a prone position and give him ten pushups. I was doing pushups in the parking lot of the Welcome Center! I was not doing well. With each pushup I would yell out, "One Drill Sergeant, two Drill Sergeant," etc.

The guy standing next to me thought this was amusing and had a smirk on his face. The Drill Sergeant saw this smirk and quickly turned his wrath on him. He ordered the young man to give him twenty pushups.

The young trainee objected with the lackluster excuse, "But I didn't do anything!"

The Drill Sergeant retorted, "You didn't do anything, *Drill Sergeant*." We immediately became friends, because misery loves company. Later on, we found out the best weapon you could have in your arsenal was silence, unless you were addressed by one of the cadre. You might also want to have a blank, motionless face. I asked myself, *What have I done enlisting in the Army?* I would ask myself this many times over the course of the next three years.

After we were processed, we all got haircuts and everyone looked around at each other, not recognizing anyone. We looked like a bunch of axe murderers. From haircuts we went to clothing issue. We walked into the largest clothing warehouse I had ever seen. People were yelling at us, "What size pants do you wear? What size shirt do you wear?"

We would say things like, "I don't know, my mom knows, give her a call." If you didn't know, the Army would guess, and they didn't guess too well. Everything was too baggy. Everything on me was too baggy in the legs, too baggy in the waist, too baggy in the ass, because I had no ass.

We all struggled with the weight of our new wardrobe. Some of us managed to stuff all the clothing into what they called a "duffle bag." I figured this was all the clothing I would ever need or want. Being from a family of nine kids, I was always getting hand-me-downs. My parents were products of the Depression of the twenties and thirties, and they impressed their thinking on us. We double-timed to the barracks and quickly got acclimated to what would be our new home for the next eight weeks.

Each trainee was issued a wall locker, a foot locker, and a bed. My, my, my—my very own Army pieces of furniture. I didn't have to share it with anyone. *Except for some yelling and screaming from the Drill Sergeants, this might not be a bad gig.* But of course, you change your mind every fifteen minutes in the Army. It's a soldier's right. Now it was time for chow, and they made us run double-time to a place called the mess hall.

This name really worried me: a "mess hall." My stomach was growling so much, it was winning the battle over my vision of a mess hall. There was a line to get into the mess hall and another line inside. Everywhere you went in the Army there was a line. There is a theory that you have to hurry up and wait. Once I got to the hot table, I studied all the available selections: roast beef, chicken, vegetables, potatoes, corn. I decided to have a little of everything, even dessert. The mess hall had a milk machine, and two little signs that read "White Milk" and "Chocolate Milk." I was surprised and elated that they had chocolate milk. So I put my glass under the spigot and all I got was white milk. I called the assistant cook over and told him I wanted chocolate milk.

"Trainees don't get chocolate milk," he said.

"The sign says chocolate milk," I told him.

"Trainees don't get chocolate milk till the last day of Basic Training."

"Well, now I have something to look forward to, don't I?"

I realized I was making another enemy and I backed off; besides, the man was a cook. No telling what he could do to me.

I sat down at a long table with five other guys with the idea of enjoying a big meal and having dessert and coffee and smoking a cigarette and just generally kicking back. No such luck.

A Drill Sergeant barked, "You have three minutes to eat and get out!" In the Army, you learn how to eat fast and smoke like a chimney.

After all this marching and running it was time to check out the bathrooms, but in the Army they called it the "latrine." Why, I don't know. If you look it up in the dictionary it simply means "a hole in the ground." I walked into the latrine and to my horror I saw the oddest sight I had ever seen.

There were eight toilets in a row, with no walls separating them. I turned to a guy and said, "Where are the stalls?"

He looked at me with a stupid grin on his face and said, "There aren't any."

I told him, "Look, all I need is three walls, a rickety door, and a cheap bolt lock in order to pinch a loaf. Throw in some bawdy graffiti on the walls and I can really enjoy myself."

Seven guys chimed in and said, "There ain't any!" So I decided to suck it up, sit down, and have a group poop. I noticed they were all reading a section of newspaper. I asked if I could have a section and they gave me one. I dropped my pants and got all nestled in. Nothing looks more ridiculous than eight men sitting on toilets with their pants down around their ankles. More unnerving was the fact that each man's knee touched the knee of the man sitting next to him.

I opened up my section of the newspaper and found out it was the obituaries. *Oh great, I'm reading about deaths of people I don't even know: Bill Dawson of Clarksville, Tennessee, died of a massive heart attack while raking his lawn. Oh God! Is this where my life has gone?* As it turned out, I had to go to the dispensary and they put a torpedo up my yoo-hoo (also called a stool softener). After that started working, I rejoined my fellow soldiers in the latrine, pants down, knees knocking, and read the editorial page.

We all hunkered down for the night; it had been a big day and we were all pretty tired and getting used to our new life. Besides, we were all tired of walking around in our underwear. No robes, no slippers, and no pajamas. I got into the top bunk. When you're six-foot-seven you're halfway up there anyways.

The guy in the lower bunk was a Mormon named Gary: nice fellow, big smile, with a long drawl when he spoke. I asked him if he wanted a cigarette but he said no thanks, he didn't smoke or drink or dance.

I asked him, "How do you woo a woman then? Those are the three things you need in your arsenal. I mean, women love men who can dance." There were some guys who could just flat out dance. They had no problem finding women.

Gary told me, "We just start courting women within our religion and then we get married, and if we want, we can have another wife."

I said, "Whoa, wait a minute, are you telling me you can have two wives?"

He responded in that long drawl, "Ooorr mooorrre." This really got my attention.

I asked, "So, theoretically, you could have six wives and go to bed with a different wife every night for six nights?"

He looked at me with a puzzled look on his face and said, "Yes, you could, but you would have to rest on the seventh day because you would be pooped."

I responded with, "Even God rested on the seventh."

He said, "Who would want to do such a thing?"

This time it was my turn to look puzzled. Why wouldn't you want to do such a feat if you could? "Well," I said, "let me ask you this. If you wanted another wife, would you have to take the homely girls or could you still take the pretty girls?" He said it didn't matter, they were all beautiful to him. I said, "No, seriously, do the homely guys have to marry the homely girls and the cool guys marry the pretty girls? No more wining, dining, or begging. I think you Mormons are on to something. Well, tell me more about it tomorrow."

I started drifting off to sleep and I could hear guys sniffling and whimpering because they missed their mommies and daddies or girlfriends. Me, I was just trying to figure out how I was going to get six Mormon wives into a 1963 Corvette.

The beds in the Army were too short. In fact, most beds were too short for my long legs. There was no room to stretch them out. At this time I was six-foot-seven and prone to leg cramps. When I was at home I would get these terrible charley horses and wake up screaming for my mom. One night I was sleeping in the barracks and I had another one. I started yelling for my mom. Suddenly the Assistant Drill Sergeant was standing by my bunk, staring at me, wanting to know what the problem was.

I told him, "I get these charley horses and my mom rubs them out for me."

He retorted, "Do I look like your mom?" I said no. Then he said, "Do you think I'm going to rub your leg?"

I replied, "Wouldja?"

Once again that booming voice came out: "Everybody get to sleep!" Boy, did I take a lot of shit from the guys after that.

Suddenly I was awakened from a sound sleep by a horrendous noise which sounded like somebody beating on a garbage can. Somebody was beating on a garbage can! It was the ungodly hour of 5:00 a.m. They were yelling at us to get up, get dressed, and get outside. This was our routine for the next eight weeks. Up early and running in formation and running to the chow hall, more exercise and marching and running to the mess hall. In between running and eating we had classes on hand-to-hand combat, chemical warfare, and infantry tactics.

One of the most popular exercises was pugil sticks. You used a stick with padding on the ends and you got to wear a football helmet. Then you beat the hell out of each other, taking your aggression and frustration out on another guy, and nobody got hurt. Everybody loved it and everybody wanted to do it again.

I only enjoyed two training classes in Basic; one was the grenade pits, and the other was the rifle range. These two operations are very dangerous and could be fatal. Everyone was focused when it came to these. One day you're driving around in your car, hanging out with friends, trying to find something to do, and the next day you're holding a one-pound explosive device in your hand capable of killing or injuring three to four people.

The training cadre performed an exercise with balloons, putting them in a thirty-foot circle and throwing a hand grenade into the middle of the circle. We watched from a distance and looked on in horror as the grenade exploded; every balloon popped. The military is the largest on-the-job training organization in the world. If you don't know how, they will teach you. Getting through the grenade exercise was pretty cool and most of us enjoyed it.

The next exercise was the rifle range. Isn't this a scary thought? One hundred guys you don't know, who have never handled an assault rifle, much less seen one, all holding a loaded weapon.

This was not like playing war in your backyard or popping off your Daisy Pump-Action BB gun. To be a good marksman, you have to put a lot of thought into what you're doing. You have to "zero your weapon in." This means adjusting the sight to the left or right in a nice shot group. It should also be noted that you have to control your emotions and heart rate. When shooting at silhouetted targets, most likely everyone can control their emotions, heart rate, and breathing. When you get into combat, it's another story.

One of the most important jobs was tearing the weapon down, cleaning it, and putting it back together. It seemed like the guys from Tennessee and Kentucky were really good at shooting and maintaining their M-14s. If anybody invaded the hills of Kentucky or Tennessee they would have a huge problem. Every man had to qualify with an M-14 or M-16 assault rifle, no matter what job you had in the Army. Everyone was a basic infantryman.

As Basic Training was winding down, you could start to see little changes in each man. The biggest change was that you were stronger and had more stamina. The second change was that you were more organized: a place for everything and everything in its place. The third change was that you were more conscious of your grooming and cleanliness. The fourth change was the growth of confidence and self-worth. Sometimes this led to cockiness and an overbearing attitude, but with a little counseling this could be managed.

Graduation day was upon us and everyone was busy pressing their class A uniforms, shining their dress shoes, getting last minute haircuts, shining their brass. It was time to get into the last formation of Basic Training and pass in review in front of our brigade commanders and battalion commanders. Eight weeks of marching, running, exercising, rifle range, hand-to-hand combat, bayonets, chemical warfare, and health classes had come to an end. Delta 4-1 passed in review, smartly saluted the commanders, and waited to be inspected in four ranks. Eight weeks ago we didn't know what a rank was. After it was all over we threw our head covers up in the air and congratulated each other.

We returned to the barracks and waited for orders to our new duty stations. As the orders came in, small groups of guys would say their goodbyes, not knowing if we would ever see each other again. Some were going to infantry school, some were going to artillery school, and some were going to armor tank school. They were going all over the United States. I was the last one to leave. My orders were coming in the next day, so I had to sleep in the barracks all by myself that night. That was all right, because I could finally sit on an end toilet, smoke cigarettes, and read the whole paper. The next morning, the Drill Sergeant woke me up and told me to get up. I had a plane to catch to Fort Eustis, Virginia, home of the U.S. Army School for Aviation. The Army even gave me a voucher for plane fare to Newport News.

As I got into the taxi, a new batch of recruits was coming in. They looked like a mob, milling around the parking lot with no direction. It reminded me of a gaggle of geese looking for the wolf to come attack them. The wolves came, two of them with Smokey the Bear hats on. I knew what was going to happen next, and got into the taxi and smiled to myself.

3

FORT EUSTIS, VIRGINIA

I CHECKED INTO THE ORDERLY ROOM AT THE TRAINING BRIGADE and was escorted to the barracks. I was moderately surprised at the condition of the barracks. They were one-story buildings in the shape of an H, with the cross section being the latrine and showers. The rooms were two-man cubicles with two bunks, two foot lockers, two wall lockers, and, to my shock and awe, two desks and two study lamps. This told me two things: the Army was serious about teaching and serious about me learning. We did have Platoon Sergeants. Their main goal was to make sure we focused on classroom study and practical exercise on the aircraft.

The first day of school was an introductory flight in a CH-47 Chinook. This was the aircraft on which we would be training. We had to get used to flying long hours. This was going to be our job in the Army. We would be crewmembers, perform missions, and service and maintain the aircraft. They told us most of us would get sick and throw up. Of course, we didn't believe them. We strapped on our helmets and buckled in. We taxied down the flight line and, from a rolling start, we took off. It was just like I had dreamed it would be. We all were grinning ear to ear. It was a good thing our mouths were open, because the vomit needed to go someplace. The place it went to was an old Folgers coffee can. To this day I do not save coffee cans because it reminds me of this.

We had manuals on flight hydraulics, prop and rotor, engine repair, electrical systems, utility hydraulic systems, transmission systems, avionics, and fuel cell systems. I thought to myself, *There is no way we can learn all this stuff.* The school brigade was run more like a military school, and the emphasis was on learning and no fooling around.

After four weeks of classroom and practical exercise, we finally got a weekend pass. The pass was only good for a two hundred mile radius. That meant Baltimore or Washington, D.C. We chose Baltimore. We all chipped in for a downtown hotel room—eight guys in one large room.

As it turned out, there were a couple of conventions going on; that's where all the women were. It was our duty to liberate the women from the old men in the weird hats with the tassels. Naturally there was plenty of liquor involved.

Somebody got the bright idea to get tattoos. In those days you could get a tattoo while being under the influence. We summoned up the courage to go down to the tattoo parlor in the seediest part of town. I was all set for a beautiful set of wings on my arm, but as I looked on in horror, watching my fellow classmates getting their arms punctured a thousand times, I quickly changed my mind. So did three other guys. The others tried to persuade me with more liquor and beer; they couldn't pour enough down me to change my mind. We took the Greyhound back to Ft. Eustis, four of us nursing their arms and four of us nursing our heads, and all dead tired.

The next morning we all got into formation and the Platoon

Sergeant barked at us: "I hope you enjoyed your weekend pass. How many got drunk?" We all raised our hands. "How many got tattoos?" Four guys raised their hands. "How many got laid?" One guy raised his hand. The Platoon Sergeant looked at him with a glare and said, "You're lying. How many have to go to the dispensary because of those lousy tattoos?" Four guys raised their hands because the tattoos had started to run and bleed. Eventually our heads cleared, the tattoos healed up, and we started the last phase of school, which was the longest one.

We got into a routine of flying and working on the CH-47. Time was going by faster now; we got one more weekend pass before graduation and all of us went to Washington, D.C. It was pretty much more of the same: drinking, women, and raising Cain.

Finally, the time had come for graduation. We donned our dress khakis and paraded before the brigade commander. He made a short speech and wished us well. They presented us with diplomas. We threw our head covers in the air and congratulated each other. We all waited in anguish for our orders, which would send us all over the world. We were all packed, ready to go. If they sent you home, that meant you were going to Vietnam. The first orders were delivered and about eight guys were going to Germany, Spain, Italy, and Korea. The rest of us were going home, but not for long.

4

VIETNAM

Y FIRST IMPRESSIONS OF VIETNAM WERE NOT GOOD. It was smelly and god-awful hot. The heat was unrelenting. I landed in Nha Trang and then I caught a loch (Light Observation Helicopter) to Pleiku. This was going to be my permanent duty station, with the 179th AVN Co.

I reported to the orderly room and was told to wait, and then to go into the company commander's office. I walked briskly into his office, stopped and clicked my heels, and saluted and waited for the return salute. He saluted me and put me at ease. I reported as ordered and he welcomed me into the unit. I blurted out that I was ready for my Chinook—eager and ready. A wry smile came over his face and he thanked me for my eagerness, but he said the United States Army was not going to give a one million dollar aircraft to an inexperienced Pfc. fresh out of Chinook school. Of course, I was crushed. This was what I had trained for and this was what I wanted. The only answer I could manage to get out was, "Oh."

I was escorted out and shown where the flight platoon barracks were. My roommate was a guy named Homer Goodfellow. I also met my Platoon Sergeant, named Loenmeyer. He got me outfitted with new flight uniforms, a helmet, and combat gear. I was assigned a hooch maid. She was to clean my uniforms, shine my shoes, make my bed, and clean the room. For all of this I paid her six dollars a month. I was assigned to Chinook 006 as a door gunner. I was disappointed, but at least I was flying and making flight pay and hazardous duty pay. I made a vow that if I ever saw that Army recruiter again I was gonna beat his ass.

The very next morning, I was awoken by the CQ (Charge of Quarters). He told me I had a mission. I looked at my watch. It was five thirty in the morning; nobody flies at that hour.

He said, "On your feet and get dressed." I got dressed, ate breakfast, and followed a bunch of guys to the flight line. I met the flight engineer, Don Crandall, and the crew chief, a guy named Carson. The flight engineer told me to get the M-60 machine guns and two thousand rounds of ammo, clean the windshield, sweep the ramp, and to do it quickly. I was going on my first mission, to resupply a firebase on the Cambodian border. I was really ready for this mission. I installed the guns and completed all my assignments.

The pilots started the engines. The blades were turning and we taxied down the runway, and I can honestly tell you it was the best high I ever had. We picked up a sling load out of Camp Holloway and headed for a firebase near Khartoum. We had to run through a valley and then up to the firebase. We kept running down the valley, which is a bad thing to do because the Viet Cong could set up an ambush, which they did.

I could see the lead ship take ground fire, so we were sure we were gonna get hit, and we did. But not for very long, because we opened up on them before we got into their range. I put down a barrage of fire, about four hundred rounds all told. That's a lot of rounds, considering that we were doing 150 knots. When we got back Crandall said that I had done a good job but I had probably warped the barrel of the M-60. I was supposed to fire in bursts of three or four. He was right.

I got back to my hooch and everyone said I got my cherry busted, which meant I had seen combat for the first time and did well. I was really high from my first mission, but I had a few beers anyway. I settled in as a gunner for about a month. I then became a crew chief on another aircraft, and a month after that I was starting to fill in as a flight engineer if one wanted a day off. I didn't have my own ship yet, and I was starting to wonder.

Then, one day, this beautiful new ship was delivered. It was a reconditioned B model made into a Super C with new and more powerful Lycoming engines. We all wondered who was gonna get this fast and powerful beast. Well, it went to me. It was worth the wait. Everything was new on her and she had the best of everything. All I needed was a crew.

I handpicked a crew chief, named DJ Blaney, and a gunner from the 189th, Ken Mathers. We installed armor plating and got her ready for combat duty. We started doing resupply missions and combat assaults near the Cambodian border. These missions started getting worse and worse. They were taking their toll on the aircraft and the crew. We just kept flying. We were getting fired on; we would return fire, hoping to silence the enemy's guns.

Some of the missions were...unusual. Once, we flew into Cambodia to evacuate refugees fleeing NVA (North Vietnamese Army) regulars. There must have been eighteen Chinooks participating in this mission. We landed in a large field. All we saw were woman and children waiting to be airlifted out to safety. American ground troops were not allowed to be in Cambodia, only aviation.

This was a big change for us. We had to arm ourselves to the teeth and assume an offensive roll, and protect our ships and the refugees. Tensions were high and everyone was on edge. We were landing very fast and creating a buffer between the refugees and the NVA. Cobra gunships strafed the area while the refugees boarded the Chinooks. Many times the NVA got through the buffer zone. Then it was up to us to stop them. We shot everything we had: M-16s, M-60s, and M-79s. We had to shoot over the heads of the refugees to hit the NVA.

This was very difficult, but finally there was a lull in the fighting. We took advantage and started loading women and children into the Chinooks. We would carry them in our arms if we had to. In all the confusion, we hadn't noticed there were no men. No husbands for the women and no fathers for the children. I thought this to be very strange, and I started asking questions. I got two different answers: the males were hauled off by the NVA, or they were killed by the NVA.

The first load was ready to go and we pulled out of Cambodia and headed for Vietnam. I noticed that the women were in a state of shock. The only thing I could do was pass out water and rations, because they had not eaten for days. We finally landed at a makeshift landing strip and unloaded the refugees. As the woman and children departed the Chinook, they would touch my arm and try to say something, which I couldn't understand.

We flew back to Cambodia and picked up another load and did this for the rest of the day. We picked up the last load near dark and raced back to Vietnam. I sat back on the Chinook near the ramp and pulled out a cigarette and reflected on this mission. It was one of those missions where you felt good about completing it because you had actually helped somebody. Maybe, just maybe, we saved a life or two; on the other hand, the refugees had lost husbands and homes and perhaps a country—all in one day.

The people of the United States never heard of this operation. The war correspondents never picked up on this at all. Whenever

I run into a war protester and he professes to know about the war, the first question I ask him is, "When were you there?" The answer is usually the same. He was never there. My answer is always the same, too. You should shut up and be quiet. This can lead to a confrontation, which is fine with me.

We actually did more missions like this in Laos and Vietnam. As the days went by, I could feel myself changing, and not in a good way. My drinking had increased and my temperament was edgy and irritable. After every mission, Jim Beam and soda was the order at night. This was what we called self-medication. I knew I needed time off; I just didn't know how to ask for it. Finally monsoon season came. It's the rainy season. You can't fly in dark, rainy weather. We all finally caught up on our sleep and rest. After a week of monsoons, we were off and running again. We were doing combat assaults, resupply, and night flare duty. My ship was taking a beating, riddled with bullet and shrapnel holes, and I was starting to take it personally.

So I decided to give the ship a name. What I really wanted to do was to get some good karma so I called the ship *Chicago Transit.* I thought it would give the ship its own identity and spirit. I was from Chicago and the Chicago Transit Authority (which later shortened its name to just "Chicago") was my favorite band, and if the news ever took a picture of the ship, maybe folks back home would cheer us on. I was grasping at straws. My crew probably thought I was nuts, but they never said a word. For a while this karma thing seemed to work, but wouldn't you know it, we soon had to fly into the Ashau valley.

****

We came from a high altitude and broke through the clouds into the valley. The valley was dark and bits of vapor streamed off our blades. I thought we were too low, because our blades were too close to the rocks and the side of the valley wall. I thought to myself that we were set up for an ambush. The Ashau valley gave me a bad feeling, like death had happened in this place before, and a lot of it. We climbed to get to the firebase. The bad thing was that the sling load was still covered in the clouds. The controller from the pathfinders had to talk us down into the landing zone. It seemed like it took ten minutes to get the load on the ground, but as soon as I released the load we banked left and climbed out of the fog and into sunshine. I let my guard down, breathed a sigh of relief, and reached for a Marlboro and lit it.

All of a sudden I heard rat-tat, rat-tat, rat-tat. I looked down and saw that holes were appearing in the floor of my helicopter. I rolled myself to the left and then to the right, just missing the rounds coming up through the floor. Both gunners opened up right away. I immediately threw two grenades out the window as I was yelling and cursing and damning. I emptied two magazines from my M-16 into the dense fog in the valley below. I was angry and pissed off, and every emotion was running through my body. I really don't know why I was so angry. We had been shot up before. I just lost my cool, and it wouldn't happen again. I had also let my guard down. I vowed that the next time we flew into the valley we would be ready. Just by chance, we came by an M-79 grenade launcher with ten grenades. I thought this would be a good weapon to have onboard, and it was.

We returned to base camp, which was Camp Holloway. I retreated into my hooch, pouring myself a Jim Beam and soda. Most of the flight platoon guys unwound after a mission. We were a very tight group of guys, but the one thing you didn't talk about was fear or being afraid. It's that bravado thing that men have. Some guys could take a lot of trauma, which is another name for combat.

I found out your close friends kind of held you together. It could be somebody on your crew or a fellow flight engineer. In my case, it was a senior pilot with whom I flew who mentored me through my tour of Vietnam. His name was CWO Dillard and he was on his second tour. I met him during my second month in Vietnam when I was a gunner on his ship. At first I thought he was overbearing and loud, but whenever he could, he bolstered my attitude. Sometimes he was gentle, other times firm, and sometimes he yelled like a madman to get his point across. Everyone needs somebody to put things in perspective. I think we all needed a mental twitch from time to time.

****

In January of 1971, things really started hopping. We were called into formation and told to pack up our gear. We were moving up north to PhuBai to support the 101st Airborne in Operation Dewey Canyon and Lamson 719 with the ARVN (Army of the Republic of Vietnam). The campaign was designed to be an all-aviation and ARVN infantry push into Laos as far as Techcopone.

Once there, all supply lines and routes were to be destroyed. No American ground forces were allowed. The American 101st Airborne had to wait at the border. This made me a little nervous. I would have preferred an American infantry division as the main probing force. We started flying sixteen hours a day, inserting ARVN troops, artillery ammo, and food and drink into Laos. This went on for about a month. Then it was time to pull everyone out.

The NVA counterattacked as the ARVN was pulling out. We were sent in to pick up casualties. We landed OK on the north side of a temporary firebase. As we were loading the wounded we came under intense mortar and small arms fire. We were fully loaded with wounded and we started raising the ramp. I told the pilot that more wanted to board the ship. We could only take sixty passengers. The pilot advised that we were fully loaded and ordered me to kick people off the ramp so we could take off. We started pushing the ARVN soldiers off the aircraft.

The mortars kept getting closer, hitting the ARVN soldiers. By staying too long on the ground, we were creating casualties. We grabbed two wounded soldiers and put them in the Chinook. The rest of the soldiers were begging us to let them come on board. We pushed them off the ramp and took off. I ran out of bandages and sulfa powder. We never had any morphine. I used old rags I had found to clean up oil spills as bandages. We landed at the nearest M.A.S.H. unit and unloaded the wounded.

As we left the hospital pad, we lost our #2 engine. We made an emergency landing in Khe Sanh and had to repair a broken engine line. We made it back safely to base camp and at daylight I inspected the aircraft. I counted forty-three holes in her from mortar shrapnel. The barrels on the M-60s were warped. The technicians from rotor and frame repaired the holes in one day and we got new machine guns and guess what? We were up and running the next day.

The normal routine for us going into a hot LZ (landing zone) was to be escorted by Huey gunships or Cobra gunships. I never liked that logic, because we could outrun the gunships. A Super Chinook could cruise at 150 knots, no problem. The gunships could only cruise at maybe 130 knots. We had to slow up so the gunships could escort us in. Once, as we were heading into a firebase in Laos, the gunship next to us was hit by an RPG (Rocket Propelled Grenade). Her tail rotor was shot to hell. We looked on in horror as she spun down to the ground, exploding on impact.

Our pilots knew what was going on and they beeped the engines up, dropped the nose, and before we knew it, we outflew our coverage and were on our own. We came into the firebase too fast and barely got our load off. We knew they were going to catch us coming out of the valley, but this time we unloaded on them first. Both gunners laid down suppressing fire as I was pumping out grenades with the launcher. We got out of there and left a lasting impression.

When we returned to base camp, we started thinking more about the guys who were shot down. Chinook guys and Huey guys go to the same schools at Ft. Eustis, VA. We almost always knew each other. When one died, a little bit of us died with him.

This Laos campaign was now in its third month and it was taking its toll on us mentally and physically. I quit writing home to my parents and friends because there was just nothing good to say. Really, what do you say? My mother had enough and contacted the Red Cross and they contacted the company commander of the 179th Aviation Co. He summoned me to his office and locked my heels and told me to write a letter to my parents in front of him.

I refuted him and asked, "And tell them what?" You can almost call an officer a horse's ass if you put the word "sir" on the end of that. We spared verbally, getting nowhere.

He put his hand firmly on my shoulder and said, "You ask about your family and you lie about yourself. It's what we do." *WOW. That was heavy. I guess I know why he's a major and I am a lowly SP/5. He has the pearls of wisdom that someday I will have.* I sat down in front of him and promptly wrote a two-page letter. I mailed it off and saluted and left his office. As I left his office and walked across the company area I thought to myself, *He's not such a bad guy after all.*

I was at my lowest point and I was looking for ways to boost my morale. I started playing basketball and touch football and throwing horseshoes. Instead of laying around thinking about

how bad things were, it was better to do sports and recreation.
This worked for a while, but sooner or later you had to get away
from the daily grind of combat and flying. One day I came off
the flight line and I was met by the company clerk and he
informed me that my travel orders for R&R had come in.

"Where to?"

"Australia."

I yelped and yelled, "When, when, when?"

"First thing in the morning."

5

R & R: AUSTRALIA

I RAN TO MY HOOCH AND STARTED PACKING MY BAGS. I had about
$800 to spend for the week. I caught a loch to Cam Rahn Bay
and boarded a 737 to Sydney, Australia, a long flight. I had no
particular loyalties to any woman back in the States, so I was a
free agent, so to speak. I planned on exercising my options for
the full week.

R&R stands for "Rest and Recreation." I planned on resting
and recreating as much as possible, and I did. The Aussie women
loved listening to my accent and I loved listening to theirs. I saw
the sights, ate great food, drank and danced the night away. I was
really enjoying my stay, and one night I was with a group of
Australian and British soldiers down at the Kings Cross section
of old Sydney. This area was a very popular place for nighttime
entertainment.

We were drinking and dancing with some of Australia's finest
women. I failed to notice that the club was running a tab on our
table. After about three hours of drinking and dancing, they

delivered the tab to the table. We all glanced at the tab and were awestruck by how the size of the check had gotten so big in such a short time. I was seriously wondering how we were going to pay the check. Without further ado, a short private from the Australian army sitting at our table announced he was going to pay the check. We all breathed a sigh of relief and cheered him and shook his hand.

The Australian private took the check in hand, looked at it, and climbed up on a chair and starting making an announcement:

"Here, here!! All you British blokes. I have something to say."

The British soldiers responded: "Well, out with it man, out with it."

The Australians urged him on: "Tell 'em, mate; tell 'em."

"Well, you know that Queen of yours? Well, last night she sucked on my wanger and she enjoyed it very much." The British did not take this well. They rushed the Australians and there was a calamity of fighting and chair throwing.

My fellow Americans and I decided that for once this was not our fight, and we left the night club with our dates. The Australian soldiers had more balls than money, so they had decided to create a diversion so we could get away. It was a common tactic used to get out of paying the check. We also took their women. The next morning, I went down for breakfast and there they all were, having breakfast and a good old time.

****

One night I was entertaining a young lady from Malaysia. I know I said I wasn't going to interact with any more Asian women but this one was drop-dead gorgeous. We were in my room having a cocktail when the phone rang. I answered and spoke with Glen Turnbolt, a nice guy from Wyoming. We flew in to Sydney together from Viet Nam.

"Hi Glen, how's it going?" I said

"Well, I have this problem maybe you could help me with," he said.

"Sure, Glen, what's your problem? And make it fast 'cause I have a young lady here and we are just getting started."

"I have a young lady here too; one of Australia's many fine women."

"That's good, what's next?"

Glen said, "Well Tommy I have a predicament. The lady in question is willing to have any kind of sex with me if I can recite the Gettysburg Address."

I looked down at the receiver of the phone and asked Glen, "Are you kidding?"

"I am not; as God is my witness, this is for real. Now Tommy, I know for a fact you know some of the Gettysburg Address 'cause I heard you recite it in a bar in Pleiku."

It was no secret I used to earn drinks by reciting the Gettysburg Address and the Preamble to the United States Constitution. When bartenders got bored and wanted to entertain the patrons they would challenge anyone to recite the Gettysburg Address. Usually no one knew it. But I did. The reward was usually drinks on the house.

I said, "All right, all right, I'll say it. But you won't remember it."

He said, "It's ok, you just say it one sentence at a time and I'll repeat it to her one sentence at a time."

"Ok let's do it. Are you ready?"

Glen said he was ready. I had this image in my mind of Glen with the phone to his ear and his BVDs down around his ankles. I looked at my date. She was wondering what was going on. She kept crossing and uncrossing her legs, which drove me crazy. I think this is very sexy when women do this. I told her with a wry smile this wouldn't take long and she might even get a history lesson. She rolled her eyes and crossed her legs again. I yelled to Glen, "Are you ready?" and he responded, "We are in position."

I began: "Four score and seven years ago..." And he repeated: "Four scores and seven years ago..."

"Our fathers brought forth on this continent..." And he repeated: "Our fathers brought for on this continent."

"A new nation..."

"A new nation..."

"Conceived in liberty and dedicated to the proposition that all men are created equal..."

"We have the liberty to conceive and be propositioned by all men equally..."

I interrupted and said, "No, that's not correct."

He said, "Keep going, its working; just keep going."

I continued: "We are now engaged in a great civil war..."

"We have to be civil in a war..."

I shook my head, but I kept going. "Testing whether that nation or any nation so conceived and so dedicated can long endure..."

"A nation has to test to conceive in order to endure..." Glen started yelling into the phone, "It's working! You can stop now. I'll take it from here."

I ended with, "I'm glad I could be of assistance. The next time you might try the Constitution or the Bill of Rights."

"You mean the constitution from where?" he said.

"Usually the United States Constitution."

"Oh that one, yeah I remember hearing about that one. Refresh my memory again. How does it go?"

"You know, 'We the people of the United States in order to perform a more perfect union...' blah, blah." Glen hung up on me and went back to his conquest courtesy of Abe Lincoln and me. As I think about it, Glen is the only guy I know who got an American history patriotic hump.

The next morning I paid for a cab for my date and joined my fellow soldiers for breakfast in the hotel restaurant. I joined two Americans and two Aussies. We ordered steak and eggs. Glen came down and joined us. He was looking very tired but happy. I asked him how the rest of the night went. Glen said, "Well, guys, a real gentleman never tells, but I'm not a gentleman so I will tell you."

The Aussies and I leaned forward in our chairs anticipating a good tale. Glen started slow and deliberate using his slow Western drawl. "Well, Tommy, you know how you suggested the Constitution?"

I shook my head in agreement and said, "Then what?"

Glen said, "To my amazement I recited the whole Constitution of the United States. That girl just went crazy. She loved hearing that stuff."

I said, "So it worked?"

Glen said, "Hell yes! It worked so well I got sex all night." Even the Aussies looked surprised. "I haven't had sex all night since, I guess I've never had sex all night." I looked at Glen, then at the Aussies, and back to Glen.

"Tell me, Glen, how did you know the Constitution?" He said, "Well it just came back to me because I must have learned it in eighth grade."

I said, "Glen why don't you recite it now for us?" Glen said he would be glad to but he wasn't motivated like he was last night. I said, "We understand, Glen, just give us a paragraph or two."

He said, "All right here goes: We the people of the United States in order to promote unions, provide defense, protect the welfare system, ask not what your country can do for you, ask what you can do for your county but do it first. Remember its Tippecanoe and Tyler too. For truth, justice, and the American way."

There was a moment of silence and then a mock standing ovation. I looked at Glen and said, "And that worked?" Glen looked at me with a big grin and said, "All night sex."

One of the Aussies piped up and said, "Excuse me, mate. I don't know a lot about American history but what happened to the guy with the canoes?" I told the Aussie there weren't any canoes; it was just a campaign slogan. He thought it didn't make any sense. I told him he was right, but we have a saying in America: The end justifies the means.

Glen got what he wanted and therefore it worked. I made a suggestion Glen try the Declaration of Independence or the Emancipation Proclamation tonight. He wrinkled his brow and said, "Which one is that?" I explained that The Declaration of Independence told the British to stuff it and we declared our freedom from them. And the Emancipation Proclamation outlawed slavery—even sex slavery. Glen spoke softly and said, "No sex slavery, huh? I suppose we enforce that one regularly?"

"We enforce all of them," I said.

The next morning I bumped into Glen with his "patriotic" girlfriend. Looking over both of them, it appeared neither one had a good night's sleep; they looked tired but satisfied. The doorman waived down a taxi and the girlfriend disappeared into the morning traffic.

Glen looked like a man with a lot on his mind. He kept saying how great she was and that she might be the one. I had a habit of keeping my answers noncommittal when somebody was talking about "the one," because in my mind she couldn't be the one in such a short time.

He finally spoke what was really on his mind. "You know I've grown to like this country. I could stay here and nobody would know."

I said, "Glen, everyone would know. You would be AWOL

(Absent Without Leave). Think of this as a short vacation on Uncle Sam. Uncle Sam paid for the travel cost and we paid for the hotels, food, and any miscellaneous expenses."

Glen replied, "But I've had great sex and was shown a great time by some really very kind people."

"That's not a good reason to go AWOL. Great sex isn't love, it's just a physical activity we all enjoy. Believe me, Glen, I've thought about everything you've mentioned and you're right. What a great country Australia is. And the people are so gracious and kind."

I was having such a great time, in fact, I wasn't watching the days go by until two MPs came to my hotel room and firmly stated that it was time to board the plane back to Vietnam. Once again, I was entertaining a nice young lady. There was one Australian MP and one American MP. The Australian was really nice and said, "Sorry, mate, but you gotta go back. You can come back after your tour is over." The American MP was not so nice. He said, "Pack your bags or we'll pack 'em for you." As we glared at each other he added, "So, that's the way it's going to be." They both started pulling my clothes out of the dressers and started packing my bags. I took the clothes out of my bags and put them back into the dressers.

This went on for about two minutes, until the American MP became agitated and said, "If you don't quit that I'll rap you with this billy club."

I said, "What's that compared to where I'm going back to?"

He said, "I know, I know what you've been through, but if there's any more trouble in Australia the brass will cut off Australia as an R&R port, and this is a great place for R&R." I reluctantly agreed.

As I started packing my bags, I was thinking I'd had a good time and I wanted to come back some day. Then I looked down at the trash can near the bed and I counted all the condom wrappers in the can. I thought to myself, I had a better time than I thought. I said my goodbyes, packed my bags, and boarded the plane back to Vietnam. The real rest came from sleeping on the plane on the way to Australia and back. We landed in Cam Rahn Bay and I got on a Ranger chopper and headed back to Camp Holloway.

I was still wearing civilian clothes when I landed at the company headquarters. I immediately got into company formation. I was out of uniform. I was wearing green bellbottom jeans with a yellow stripe down the sides and a very stylish, white, long-sleeved shirt with a wide collar and pin-striping. The verbal abuse from my fellow aviators was brutal. They immediately refrained from any more abuse when I said three words: "Australian round eye." They were respectful and envious.

I went back to my hooch, changed into my flight suit, got my gear together, and walked to the flight line. The other flight engineers, crew chiefs, and gunners started yelling at me, "You got some round eye!" Word travelled fast. I smiled in agreement and boarded my ship. My crew chief and gunner were waiting to hear about my exploits in Australia. The R&R had reinvigorated me and rested my mind. Now I was ready to complete the rest of my tour of duty.

6

BACK TO VIETNAM

ONE OF THE THINGS THE WAR DID WAS disrupt people's lives. It disrupted the way things were supposed to happen, not only for military people, but also civilians. Boy doesn't meet girl, boy doesn't court girl, boy doesn't marry girl. But sometimes the strangest things happen in the middle of a war: An American soldier wanted to marry a Vietnamese girl.

Everyone knew Vietnamese women only wanted to marry G.I.s to get to the United States. I figured she was a prostitute looking for a life in the U.S. I told this guy, Bobby Ryun, "She's just using you." He didn't like that remark. I was dead set against him getting married. She was his hooch maid and she really took good care of him. She washed his clothes and made sure he ate healthy foods. I saw this and thought, *What prostitute does this?* She was more gaga than he was. Those two had it bad. I eventually changed my mind about her and so did everyone else, except the Army. They could get married by civilian authorities, but the Army would not recognize the marriage.

So, on a Sunday afternoon in November, half the company turned out for a wedding and reception, dressed in khakis or class As. We ate and drank, just like at any other wedding. What a crazy day. What a crazy war. Out of the horrors of war came a good thing. The war was all around us, but these two people were bound and determined that the war would take a back seat for one day. I think we needed that one day of normalcy to give us a rest from the everyday rigors of war and conflict.

****

Christmas came and my parents sent me a fold-up Christmas tree with about twenty lights on it. They also sent me a couple coffee cans filled with cookies and fudge. I passed them around to all the guys and wished them a Merry Christmas. I think the holidays made everyone a little homesick. The mess hall outdid itself with roast turkey and ham, mashed potatoes, and every dessert you could think of. They really put out a nice spread for us. I spent the rest of the day writing letters to home and pitching horseshoes.

The very next day we were flying around Firebase English. We were doing resupply sorties up around the DMZ. We were almost finished when we were diverted to a firebase in Laos for a casualty evacuation. The CH-47 can hold up to twenty-four stretcher cases. This was not a mission I liked, because we were not set up like a medevac Huey. We had no medical supplies on board and no medics.

The pilots started their approach to the firebase at around 150 knots, but the small firebase was getting hit with small arms fire and mortars. We were waved off three times because the firebase was in danger of getting overrun. The plan was to get us in and evac the wounded. After we were out, they could call in airstrikes or bring artillery from nearby firebases. The sun was going down so we had to get in soon. The pilots got the word and all of a sudden it was a go.

We came down from a high altitude and the helicopter felt like it was doing 180 knots. The transmissions were howling and blades were really popping. The aircraft was shaking and vibrating like I had never felt before. This was the fastest I had ever gone! I couldn't get to my seat to buckle myself in, so I grabbed the static line that ran from the front of the cabin to the rear. I said a little prayer: "Oh God, if this is where it ends so be it. I want to die looking through the cockpit over the pilot's shoulders."

The pilot looked at me and said, "Chief, we're going in fast and hard." I remember commenting to myself that these two pilots had volleyballs between their legs. I started thinking about the people who manufactured the CH-47, the Boeing Vertol Corporation, the people who assembled her and tested her. What an aircraft: fast, powerful, and well made. I saw the firebase up ahead about a mile away. I saw a small pad where we could land. We came in fast, flared our rotors, raised our nose, and dropped our rear end. Before we knew it, we were on the ground. I dropped the ramp and we started loading wounded.

We decided not to use the stretchers, instead laying the wounded on the floor of the aircraft. The pilot was screaming into my headset to hurry up. We loaded all the wounded into the aircraft.

I told the pilots, "Ramps up, ready in the rear." He pulled pitch and we got out of there. I looked at some of the wounded and I noticed that some were not looked after. The medic was busy taking care of other wounded.

I saw one ARVN soldier bleeding profusely from his back, down his legs, into his boots. I muttered to myself, "What the fuck?" He was lying there, screaming in pain, and I couldn't blame him. I motioned to the medic to give him morphine.

"He needs more than morphine," the medic said. "Help me get his clothes off and stop the bleeding." We lifted the soldier's shirt, pulled his fatigues down, and looked in horror at a fountain of blood coming out of several holes in his back and backside.

I said, "Where do we start?" I wanted to go back to my duties as a flight engineer, but the medic would have none of that. Together we spread sulfa powder and pressure bandages on the soldier. After that we put his field jacket around him and tied off the waist and the thighs. Then the medic gave him the morphine. I went back to the ramp area and lit up a Marlboro and thought to myself, *That guy ain't gonna make it.*

We landed at a M.A.S.H. unit at Khe Sanh and unloaded the wounded. I asked a doctor if that guy was gonna make it.

He said, "Fifty-fifty chance. Did he lose a lot of blood?"

"Fuck yeah," I said and pointed to the floor of the Chinook.

"We'll do the best we can."

We did several more extractions that day and headed back to base camp in the dark. We landed and did preventive maintenance. I told the crew to go to chow and that I would catch up to them later. I lay down on the seats of the aircraft and thought about the day.

I started thinking about how long I could do this job, and then I thought about what normal twenty year olds were doing: going out on dates, going to dances, swimming at the beach, making out in a car, cruising in a car with the top down, speeding down Lakeshore Drive. I was considering quitting flying and serving the rest of my tour of duty on a maintenance team working on Chinooks; a nice, safe job with nobody shooting at you. I decided to talk to the company commander in the morning.

I fell asleep on the aircraft and slept for about six hours. I had slept in my flight suit so I looked pretty rumpled. I went straight to the mess hall, ate a good breakfast, and changed my clothes. I got the crew and went back out to the ship, and decided I wasn't going to quit flying and I wasn't going to quit being a flight engineer. It was the best job I had ever had. I loved this job, but I did have doubts.

Was I experiencing a little bit of cowardice, or was I actually coming to my senses? There was nobody to talk to about the mental state I was in. It must be a guy thing. We don't share with each other. So I decided to put on a good front and mask the conundrum I was in. You mask it with self-medication, such as booze and drugs; mine was bourbon. But most of all you mask it with silence and denial.

There was another weapon I used, though. It was anger. Used properly, anger could help you respond to dangerous situations. It's sort of like a controlled rage. You have to always be on guard and vigilant. This was very tiring and hard on me mentally and physically.

Most of the time we were fighting the NVA and the Viet Cong, but sometimes we had to fight our own allies, the people we were sent there to help. The ARVNs were notorious for stealing our equipment. I was always on guard with these people. One day we had a bunch of ARVNs unloading rations off the aircraft, when I spotted an ARVN soldier stealing our flashlights and the pilots' cameras. He had shoved them down his shirt and started walking off the aircraft. I stopped him at the ramp and told him to hand over the flashlight and cameras. He acted like he didn't understand. I made him understand. I tore open his shirt and out dropped flashlights, a camera, and some tools. I looked at everything but didn't say a word. I hit that little gook so hard his front teeth folded back into his mouth. Some MACV (Military Assistance Command Vietnam) guy pulled that little turd out of there. The pilots wanted to press charges against him, but decided not to.

There was another faction of the Vietnamese population that caused trouble. They were called "cowboys," and they rode around on Honda 50cc motorcycles, terrorizing the law-abiding citizens. Sort of like Hell's Angels, only on Honda 50s. Most of the cowboys were draft dodgers and low-level criminals. If we ever came in contact with them, they would throw us the bird, swear at us, or cut us off if we were riding through town. Sometimes they would get brave and throw rocks at us. This was not a good thing to do.

One day we loaded up on rocks and cans of oil, whatever we could find, and drove through downtown Pleiku and waited for the cowboys to start throwing rocks. When they did, we let go with everything we had. They were really surprised and shocked we would do something like that. By and large, though, the civilians supported us most of the time.

****

The CH-47 Chinook was a tandem-rotor, twin-engine, cargo helicopter capable of carrying loads of 12,000 lbs. We carried sling loads whenever we could. We tried not to carry internal loads because if you lost an engine, you couldn't get rid of the load. With sling loads, you pressed a button and dumped the load. This happened to me as we were resupplying a firebase along the Cambodian border.

We were sling-loading a 105 howitzer when we lost the #1 engine and started falling out of the sky. The pilots tried to restart the engine. I grabbed the pistol control for the hook and calmly asked the pilot if he wanted me to dump the load.

He responded, "No, we're trying to restart the engine." We continued dropping towards the ground.

The pilots were nervously trying their best to restart the engine. I looked down through the cargo trap door and saw the earth coming up at us. This time I asked the pilot with a little more concern in my voice, "DO YOU WANT ME TO DUMP THE LOAD?!!"

The pilot finally responded, "Dump the son-of-a-bitch." I pressed the hook to open and the load came off the hook and the aircraft shot straight up and plastered me to the floor. The pilots equalized the rotor speed and we leveled off and all started breathing again.

We landed near the 105 cannon and the demo guys put a charge in the barrel and blew it clean off. There was an investigation afterwards and it was found that everything had been done by the book and all the proper procedures had been followed. After that the cannon was named "Messenger's Cannon," after me.

One thing should be noted: Whenever we flew fast or descended very quickly, or were flying very low to the ground, it was a euphoric and enjoyable experience for me. Can you imagine I was getting high off my own aircraft? I've spoken to pilots and other flight engineers and they never really said they got high off flying in Chinooks, but they did all say they loved flying them. It was the fastest and most powerful helicopter in the free world at the time.

****

Our duties also included working with Special Forces out of Kontum. The plan was that Special Forces would build a heavily fortified camp in the middle of nowhere and little villages would build up around the camp. When the villagers came under attack, they could seek protection inside the camp. (This concept dates back to the feudal system in England where the peasants and serfs would seek protection in the lord's castle in time of war.) It would be our job to land near the village, load up all the villagers, livestock, and farming equipment, and take them to the Special Forces camp, unload, and go back and do it all over again till everyone was moved in.

During this time I was in contact with the villagers and I grew to like some of them. They led a very simple life and most of them appreciated what we were doing.

The best group of people to work with we called the "Montagnards." These were the people who lived in the mountains and jungles of Vietnam. Their loyalty to the Special Forces was never questioned. We would relocate them and supply them with rice and water. When I first came into contact with the Montagnards, it was like walking into a *National Geographic* magazine. They wore loincloths only. The women dressed the same as the men. They were bare-chested and usually nursing a baby. The men hunted with crossbows and spears and were excellent scouts and guides. I guess if I have any regret about the missions I went on, it's that we didn't do enough for these people.

I remember delivering food to a village along the Laos border. It was an internal load, which we didn't like to do very often. Some of the boxes were open and I looked inside, and it was bags and bags of Uncle Ben's rice. I thought, *Why are we shipping bags of rice to Vietnam?* This land was either mountains, jungles, or rice paddies. (I never got an answer.)

One day we were coming in and we landed on the outskirts of a small village, and the pathfinders were just standing there in shock and looking numb.

I asked one pathfinder, "What's going on, is the village ready to be moved?"

He replied, "They all ran off. The people who didn't run off were killed last night. The Viet Cong came in the middle of the night and killed a couple of villagers, and the rest ran off." These people were just trying to lead a simple life as peacefully as possible; they had become casualties of this crazy Asian war.

As I walked through the village, every emotion was going through my body: shock and horror, anger, and the worst one of all, vengeance. You see, we have the guns and the weapons to exact revenge. It takes cool heads to recognize a situation that could get out of hand. This is where good leadership steps forward and advises everybody to take a breath and be professional. We had great pilots and NCOs.

I soon realized we were up against a sadistic enemy and human life was cheap. I was more resolved than ever before that my prime mission was to protect the pilots, my crewmen, and the ship. Whenever the NVA would take shots at us we made sure we responded with a volley of machine gun fire they wouldn't soon forget. It was the "Chicago way." They send one of yours to the hospital, you send two of theirs to the morgue.

****

In order to get good pilots, you needed good instructor pilots. Every company had one or two instructor pilots, and it was their job to train the rookie pilots right out of flight school. These are often called "check rides." The instructor pilots made sure every pilot was adept at emergency landing procedures, otherwise called auto rotation, sling loading operations, and flying by instruments in bad weather and zero visibility. These missions were very boring and could put you to sleep.

We were flying at around three thousand feet when all of a sudden the instructor pilot started yelling at the pilot. The instructor pilot was CW3 Rick Dillard. He was a tough but fair instructor and I trusted his judgment. The two pilots were arguing back and forth. Dillard told the pilot to get out of the cockpit and go back and sit with the crew. He did, and I was a little surprised at what was going on. I felt a little sorry for him.

So I said, "Sir, you need to get back in that cockpit and be the pilot."

He looked at me with a sheepish look and said, "He doesn't want me there."

I looked at him and said, "Well, sir, go tell him to fuck himself. You're the pilot."

I suddenly realized only one pilot was flying this aircraft. Dillard then called me on my intercom, and ordered me to the cockpit. He then ordered me to sit in the right seat and put my hands on the controls. I put my feet on the yawl pedals and my right hand on the cyclic stick.

He said, "OK, you've got the aircraft."

And I said, dumbfounded, "I do?"

"You do."

He instructed me that, if I decided to make a move, I should do it slowly.

I responded, "I think I'm gonna crap my pants."

"That's OK," he said, "but do it slowly. Let's do a right bank turn."

I said, "OK."

"Fine, now just kick a little right yawl pedal and bring the stick to the right." I instructed the crew that we were coming right and came right, and then he said, "Return to a straight course."

This was so cool! We flew for about two hours. I approached the air field at Camp Holloway. Dillard took control of the aircraft and said, "I am not gonna let you land this aircraft." I didn't argue, landing and hovering a helicopter are the hardest maneuvers to do.

This was one of the greatest moments of my military career. Too bad it had to come at the expense of another human being. It was a great experience I'll never forget. I had a fantastic view, speed, and power. It made me think, *Maybe I'm destined for a better lot in life.* I knew the two pilots had plenty to say to each other, so I had the crew lag behind so the two men could discuss their problems. I did manage to fly my own aircraft two other times, and it was as good as the first time.

****

On another occasion, I flew with Rick Dillard to Saigon for supplies for the 179th Aviation. We stopped off in Qui Nhon to refuel and eat a quick lunch at one of the snack bars. That was where the problem started. After lunch we took off for Saigon and landed there at about three o'clock, and started loading the aircraft with supplies: new flight uniforms, fatigues, sports equipment, and oh yes, what we all need, toilet paper. We also picked up some passengers to take back to Pleiku.

We were about an hour into the flight when I heard Mr. Dillard complain about stomach cramps and severe diarrhea. He was actually crapping in his pants and all over my seat cushions in the cockpit. He barked orders at me. He needed another set of flight suit pants and toilet paper. First we had to land so he could finish crapping and change clothes. We landed near a village. Dillard came racing out of the cockpit and I handed him the pants and the toilet paper. There was Dillard, crapping in some guy's field and throwing toilet paper around. He cleaned himself up and got back in the aircraft.

We took off and continued our journey back to base. All of a sudden, he had to do it again. I found another set of flight pants and another roll of toilet paper. We landed in the middle of nowhere and he got out and crapped in a field and cleaned up. We took off again and this time made it back home. Dillard took off to the dispensary. The way I figured it, he probably got dysentery from the bad food in Qui Nhon.

The people we were carrying on that trip were cherries. They came up to me and asked me if this went on all the time.

I looked at them and asked, "Does what happen all the time?"

They replied, "You know, the pilot stops in the middle of the jungle and takes a dump."

"All the time." The cherries left and the crew and I had a good laugh.

The next week I had Dillard again as one of my pilots. I walked up to him and said, "You owe me big time for last week."

He replied, "You didn't tell anyone, did you?"

I said, "No, of course not."

"Good," he said, "keep it that way." For forty-three years I never told anyone, not until now.

****

Whenever a helicopter went down it was a big deal and bells and whistles went off. A Bell UH-1 helicopter at the time of the Vietnam War cost around $250,000 and a CH-47 Chinook cost around one million dollars. There were three reasons that a helicopter went down: (1) mechanical failure, (2) pilot error, and, last but not least, my favorite, (3) you got your ass shot out of the sky. If you somehow landed the aircraft safely, you had a chance of surviving this ordeal. The skies of Vietnam were loaded with American aircraft coming to your rescue. The NVA knew this, and we knew they knew. If the NVA saw a downed UH-1 they most likely would set up an ambush, because we always came after our air crews.

Going after downed aircraft was a very hazardous duty. The Army trained teams to go in and do this dangerous work. Of course, the whole idea was to not stay on the ground too long so you could avoid the ambush and save your aircraft.

The first aircraft that were sent in to recover a downed helicopter were the Huey or Cobra gunships. They would try to draw fire from the NVA and then lay down a base of fire from mini-guns or rockets. The next to come was the air assault team to set up a security perimeter. Once the perimeter was secured, the rigging team was sent in to rig the helicopter with nylon straps so the helicopter could be extracted. At the last minute, the Chinook was called in to extract the helicopter.

When a Chinook went down, this really got people's attention. The only thing that could lift a Chinook was another Chinook, but you had to remove the blades and engines or call for a Sikorsky sky crane.

We had a saying for whenever you heard somebody bragging about their Huey's, Kiowa's, Rangers, or any helicopter. We told them, "Sooner or later you'll end up under the belly of a Chinook." This usually brought a smile to our faces. The Chinook had been known to pick up F-111 jet fighters and F-104s. So if jet jockeys got a little too big for their helmets, we always reminded them of our favorite saying.

****

I had been flying so much that I really didn't pay attention to the ringing in my ears. The only time it really bothered me was when there was no noise, like at night, and when I would try to drop off to sleep. Not only would I crew my own ship, but other ships too, because we were short on flight engineers. I finally went to the flight surgeon about my ears. He looked at my ears and gave me some drops and assigned me twenty-four hours bed rest, which I gladly took. It didn't help much, but I took advantage of it anyway and slept as much as I could.

The other illness that really bothered me was dysentery. I was incapacitated for three days. This was a horrible disease that affected your stomach all the way down to your yoo-hoo. You might as well be eating your meals on the toilet. I had to replenish my liquids whenever I could because of severe dehydration.

My wisdom teeth started acting up three months before I was to go home, so I decided to have them looked at by a dentist. There was a field dentist set up on the base. I walked into this tent where the dentist was and looked at the drill sitting on a four-by-four pallet, and a dentist's chair sitting on another pallet. I was starting to get a little worried. The dentist told me to sit down in the chair and tell him what the problem was. I nervously asked him if he knew what infection was.

He responded, "Why yes, I know all about infection. Do you suspect you have an infection?"

I replied, "I might have one after I leave here." I told him my wisdom teeth were acting up. He tilted the chair backwards and took a look in my mouth and started making little "tsk, tsk" noises and muttering under his breath, "Very bad, very bad, very, very, very bad."

I said, "Doc, what's bad, what's bad?"

"Very bad very, very bad…," was his only reply.

His mannerisms reminded me of Floyd the barber in Mayberry on *The Andy Griffith Show*. He finally told me my wisdom teeth had to be cut out. *Oh yeah, I'm gonna let Floyd the barber cut my teeth out.* All of a sudden my teeth weren't hurting anymore. He told me he didn't do that sort of surgery and that an oral surgeon would have to do it. The next time a surgeon was available was in two months. I figured in three months, I would be back to the world.

I said, "OK, Doc, have a nice day. Say hi to Gomer and Aunt Bee."

"What?" he said.

"Nothing. It was just a little hometown humor." And I was out of there.

****

Sometimes after I came off a mission I had a little time to myself, and I reflected on the next day's missions. That's when I started thinking about all the people who were involved in this war: the Vietnamese, the Cambodians, the Laotians. Then I added the military forces: the armies of Vietnam, the Australians, the South Koreans, and the Americans.

This was huge. No longer was I sitting at home watching the news; I was participating in the news. I was just a tall, skinny, twenty year old from the south side of Chicago trying to make sense of this crazy Asian war. I couldn't make a difference in this war to win it or to somehow tie it. I couldn't bring both sides to the bargaining table. This is what I could do: I could protect my pilots, my crew, and my ship, and accomplish all my missions. I could do my job and service and maintain my aircraft. By doing all that, the aircraft protected everyone and the pilots and crew watched and protected me.

Most of the public was under the misconception that a soldier got up in the morning, ate breakfast, went out to the battlefield, fought for eight hours, went back for chow, slept for eight hours, and repeated this process the next day. Not true! The average Vietnam soldier fought for 245 days out of 365 days. There was some down time. During this down time you got to know your crew and pilots. Most of the pilots were really great guys. But there was one pilot who was always crabby and disagreeable. Whenever he would address me I would reply in short sentences: "Yes, sir. No, sir."

One day I observed this pilot walking down the flight line, going to his aircraft, carrying all his flight gear and an inflated rubber inner tube under his left arm.

I thought this quite odd and asked my pilots, "What's with the inner tube?" My pilots responded that the crotchety pilot had hemorrhoids so bad that whenever he sat for a long period of time he had to sit on the inner tube, allowing the hemorrhoids to have space. Hemorrhoids fill with blood and look like grapes hanging from your asshole and are very painful.

So I asked my pilots, "Is this why this guy is such a dick?"

The pilots looked at me and smiled. "Well, that explains most of it."

So I had this idea that if I could make this pilot more comfortable flying my aircraft, maybe he wouldn't be such a hard ass.

I had an old pilot's chair cushion I used for laying on the floor, and I took his inner tube and traced the width of the hole on the cushion. Then I took my knife and cut out the hole in the stuffing of the cushion about three inches deep. Then I had a terrible thought: *If I do this for this dickhead and it works, he'll want to fly with me all the time, because I have the cushion on my aircraft.* I thought about this for a little while. I decided to give him my invention and we tried it out the next day. Wouldn't you know, it worked. He was much better to get along with, but he was still a little bit of a dick.

****

There were many characters who made up the aviation company. My crew chief was a guy named DJ Blaney, a quiet sort from Texas with that long, Southern drawl I enjoyed listening to. He was like my right hand and I could always depend on him. Blaney was a young hopeful who wanted to fly helicopters for a living. He had gone through the warrant officer training program at Ft. Wolters, Texas. He'd been in a terrible car accident, broken his jaw and had to drop out of the training program. He was back to being an enlisted man and the Army had decided to send him to Vietnam as a door gunner.

Somehow he crewed on my ship and I liked the way he did his job. I asked that he be permanently assigned to my aircraft. We never had a cross word between us. When it was my turn to leave Vietnam, I would turn the ship over to him.

On the other gun was another Texas boy, Ken Mathers. He was the total opposite of Blaney, a little on the nervous side, and loved to drink too much. I would have to remind him from time to time about his duties. When he was off duty he was usually seen with a beer in his hand. While on duty, he was straight and alert. Besides, whenever we were taking fire he could lay down suppressing fire with the best of them.

He had married young, before he came to Vietnam. He had this funny habit of keeping a 9x12 photo of his wife in the bottom of his duffel bag. He argued that the picture with the frame kept the duffel bag level and square at the bottom so the bag could stand up by itself. One day, he took the picture of his wife out of the duffel bag and showed it to us. We looked at it and told him to put it back in the duffel bag.

All through my tour of Vietnam, I would meet people from all walks of life. I would spend a little time with them, then they would be gone. One of the jobs of a flight engineer was to train the people who fly on your aircraft. Training was constant, because experienced people were leaving Vietnam and new people were coming in.

The method of training went something like this: you told them, if that didn't work, you told them louder, if that didn't work, you showed them, if that didn't work, you made them do it with you watching them do it, if that didn't work, then you told them to get the fuck out of there. Then you got guys who came out of Chinook school, and you couldn't tell them anything. It kind of reminded me of somebody. Most of the time, training somebody to crew on a CH-47 Chinook was a pleasant experience. Everybody liked to fly on a helicopter, but there was more to it than flying. Flying was the end result. You had to perform daily maintenance and service and inspections, and every one hundred hours of flying time you had to perform depot maintenance. All these functions had to be performed before the aircraft was airworthy.

I had one guy who wouldn't listen and knew it all. I knew I had to change his method of thinking, so I pulled a little joke on him. On the back of the Chinook were three discharge hoses: one for excess fuel, one for oil, and one for the crew's urinary discharge station, in case you had to urinate while in flight. I asked him to tell me what was coming out of the hoses and to identify the liquid. I went into the helicopter and promptly started urinating into the hose and asked him what was coming out.

He said, "I don't know."

I said, "Is it oil?" He said no.

Then I said, "Is it fuel?" He said no.

I said, "Well, what is it?"

He put a little bit in his mouth and said, "Well, it tastes like piss."

"That was exactly right!" I said. "Not everyone knows everything. Clean the guns, sweep the floor, and clean the pilot's windshield."

This was a process of tearing down and building up and getting the person ready for the next position. On the Chinook that was crew chief and then flight engineer. The longer you kept your ship flying, the more use you were to the grunts in the field. The Chinook was a workhorse. It wasn't pretty to look at but it was powerful and fast and it's been around a long time. The United States Army has been trying to retire this aircraft for the last twenty years and they can't, because they haven't designed anything better.

7

LOOKING FOR FLYBOYS

TO WANT TO FLY IS NORMAL; TO REALLY, ACTUALLY do it is ludicrous. There is nothing aerodynamic about a helicopter. It's basically an eggbeater with a body connected to it. There were very few people who wanted to fly who could actually do it. If the pilots weren't any good, they got washed out at flight school. For the mechanics trained at Ft. Eustis, flying on the Chinook wasn't a prerequisite. When you got to Vietnam, you made the choice of whether you wanted to crew on a Chinook or stay on the ground and work on them. If you wanted to crew, you got sixty bucks extra for flight pay. For the extra pay, you got to fly hazardous missions all day and service the aircraft all night. Somewhere in there, you got to eat and sleep. To quote Joe Galloway, "We were God's lunatics."

People thought I was nuts for flying in Chinooks. Personally, I never gave it much thought. Some guys would start crewing, but then they couldn't take it. They would get sick or dizzy, but they wanted the extra money. You can't fly for the money. You have to fly cause you love it. The first couple of times I flew, I threw up in a Folgers coffee can yelling at the top of my lungs, "I love flying! I love flying!" I really did love flying. I got used to it and then motion sickness never really bothered me.

Sometimes guys from the orderly room, the mess hall, the motor pool, would ask, "So, what's it like flying?"

I would always reply, "Come fly with us and find out."

They would usually say, "Nah, just tell me what it's like."

I would then sing Franks Sinatra's song "Come Fly With Me."

There was this one kid who pestered the hell out of me for months. He wanted to ride left gun and see what it was like. He was a nice enough kid. He was in charge of the flight schedules and if you had a flight assignment, he would wake you up every morning at five o'clock.

I finally relented and said, "OK, you can fly as an observer and spend some time on the left gun. But you have to clear it with the flight platoon leader, Captain Filer. You also have to wear a flight suit and you're not gonna get paid extra flight pay for it."

I was counting on Capt. Filer saying no. I was leaving the flight line when I ran into a couple of flight engineers from my unit.

They came up to me and said, "Are you fucking nuts? You're gonna let Hooper fly left gun? He'll probably fall out of the aircraft at four thousand feet. He's too young; he's just a boy."

My answer: "We were all young when we got here, and we all needed a chance."

Just then Capt. Filer came down the flight line and asked to have a word with me. He started out softly and then boomed out, "Are you fucking nuts, letting Hooper fly left gun?"

I replied, "Sir, everyone needs a chance."

He looked at me with a quizzical look on his face and said, "Well, it's on you."

I said, "Am I to understand that you're okaying Hooper flying left gun, sir?"

He replied, "I am giving my permission."

Then it was my turn to say, "Are you fucking nuts, sir?" You can say almost anything to an officer if you put "sir" on the end of the sentence.

He said, "No, you were right; everyone needs a chance. Besides, I'll try to schedule you for a couple milk runs so you shouldn't run into too much trouble." I was halfway relieved that we were going on milk runs the next day.

The next morning we ate breakfast and set out for the flight line. There was no sign of Hooper. I guessed he must have changed his mind. *Well that's OK*, I thought to myself. *Not everyone is cut out for this job.* As we got closer to the aircraft, I saw somebody cleaning the pilots' windshield. It was Hooper! He had shown up.

Hooper came off the maintenance stand and said, "Chief, the windshield is all clean and ready to go." (The flight engineer on a Chinook is called "chief.")

I said, "Very good, Hooper; now go get two M-60 machine guns and four thousand rounds of ammo."

The pilots and I did the preflight and found everything OK. Everyone got their helmets and got to their stations. The pilot started the APU (Aircraft Preparation Unit) and said, "Ready on one."

I replied, "One is ready," and he started the #1 engine.

Then the pilot said, "Ready on two," and I replied, "Two is ready," and he started the #2 engine. When the rotors are first turning, they move slowly and the aircraft looks like it's doing a hula dance. Eventually the rotors started turning faster and they reached maximum rpms. I threw the chocks in the rear and put the ramp up.

As we started taxiing down the flight line and onto the main runway, I looked over at Hooper. I saw that smile come over his face that I'd seen before. The pilot asked if everything was clear. We cleared the pilot for takeoff and we started rolling down the runway. As we neared the end of the runway, the pilot pulled the thrust and we started gaining altitude and before you knew it, we were at three thousand feet and climbing. We were working Da Nang and the Quan Tri province.

I noticed Hooper looking out the window for any enemy movement on the ground. His eyes were constantly fixed and his eyes were bugged out. I told him to relax his eyes and close them a little, and to turn his head from side to side. If he didn't, he would have a terrific headache at the end of the day. We finished dropping our last sortie and were headed home. We would be home by dinner time and everything had gone off without a hitch.

So I lit up a congratulatory Marlboro. I was puffing away when the pilots announced over our radio that we had been diverted to Firebase English near the DMZ for an emergency sortie of 105 ammo. I thought to myself, *We just got fucked, and without a condom.* I had a real problem now. I had two experienced pilots, two experienced gunners, and one cherry gunner who wanted to shoot up the whole countryside. If I took Hooper off the gun he'd think I'd lost confidence in him. Normally I liked to have my most experienced men with me.

This time I went with the rookie and told the other gunner, Kenny Mathers, to load his M-16 with a triple banana clip and stand near Hooper. I told him to be ready: if Hooper didn't return fire, then he'd return fire with his M-16 and try not to shoot off our blades. We picked up the load in Khe Sahn and flew north to Firebase English. We put on our chicken plates (chest protector, body armor) and checked our guns. I put armor plate down on the floor near the hole where I would lay and direct the pilots to the landing zone. I walked over to Hooper and checked to see if he had his chicken plate on correctly. Hooper looked at me with a nervous smile that I understood very well; I gave him a playful punch in the arm and said, "You'll be fine."

I looked at the other guys and said, "Time to earn your money." We were now on final approach.

We came down from thirty-five hundred feet to five hundred feet but were going way too fast, because the load was swinging right to left. That's the news pilots don't like to hear, because it means you have to slow your airspeed. The load stabilized and we kept going toward the firebase. We were about half a mile from Firebase English. This was where we were the most vulnerable, and sure enough, three rounds from an AK-47 hit the battery box and the bottom of the ship. All the gunners opened up and sprayed the jungle. We got over the drop zone and I released the load and advised the pilots we were clear for flight.

Now we had to get out, but not the same way we had gone in. We banked left and started on a different course away from the drop zone and waited for the next ambush to come, but it didn't. We climbed to about four thousand feet and finally got out of range and into the clear. I checked for any damage to the aircraft. It was minimal. We removed our chicken plates and breathed a sigh of relief.

Over the radio came a message: "Thank you, shrimp boat 528, for the much needed ammo. We will see you tomorrow."

I went to the back of the aircraft near the rear window, sat down, and pulled out a Marlboro and lit up. I relaxed for a minute and thought about all the missions I'd been on. *Sooner or later they are gonna get me, and it's just a matter of time before they do.* I wondered how bad it was going to be. I was thinking way too much and I knew it. This could be very hazardous. The one thing I knew was that Mr. Beam would be waiting for me back in my room. We landed at Camp Eagle. The pilots and I did a post-flight inspection on the aircraft and everything was OK except for the holes. I called for sheet metal to repair the skin. I closed up the aircraft, disconnected the batteries, and started walking back to the flight shanty to drop off the forms. I was always the last one to leave the aircraft.

Walking ahead of me were the gunners, and they were talking about the last mission. They were talking a mile a minute about returning fire and wondering if they had got any confirmed kills. The adrenaline rush was better than you could imagine. It took a long time to come down from it. DJ and I ate dinner in the mess hall and I went to the bar and bought two cans of 7Up. I looked down to the end of the bar and there were the gunners and crew chiefs talking about the last mission. They kept adding more to the story than had actually happened. This was what happened when you added alcohol to a good story. It got better. They noticed me at the end of the bar and asked me to come over and have a drink.

I had participated in many a bullshit session where alcohol was involved. But tonight I was a little tired and I wanted some solace with a night cap. I told Hooper he had done a great job, that he had really stepped up and protected the ship, making sure the other guys could hear. The other guys looked at Hooper with a new look of respect. With that, I walked away and went to my hooch and poured me a Jim Beam over ice. I thought about writing letters home to my parents. Didn't want to do that. Maybe write to my sisters? No, didn't want to do that either. I could write my old girlfriend. We had decided to call it quits before I went overseas. The Jim Beam was getting to me, though, so I decided not to write to anyone.

I started to drift off to sleep, dreaming about driving down Ashland Avenue with all my friends, having a great time, when I was abruptly awoken from my sound sleep by Hooper. He still hadn't come down from his battle experiences of the day. At least, that's how he would tell it. He shook me from my deep sleep.

Hooper said, "I don't want anybody to know, but I have to tell you."

I said, "Tell me what, Hooper?"

"Today I was afraid. I was shaking."

"Hooper, me too," I told him.

"Not you," he said. "What are you afraid of?"

"I'm afraid we'll have mechanical failure and fall out of the sky. I'm afraid of getting shot out of the sky. I'm afraid of landing and getting ambushed. I'm afraid of the pilots and the crew getting shot, and I'm afraid of getting shot."

Hooper looked at me with a puzzled look and said, "Then why do you do it? It's not the money, is it?"

"It's not the money. It's the action. It's my drug of choice. It's only one of my afflictions."

Hooper said, "Wow, Chief, you're fucked up. Are all you flight engineers fucked up?'

I said, "Pretty much. Shut up and go to bed so I can get to sleep and do it all over again tomorrow." As Hooper left, he asked if he could fly tomorrow.

"No, I have a gunner," I said.

The other guys were right; we didn't want Hooper to get hurt, or worse yet, die. He went back to his regular duties and not another word was said about it. Hooper had his story he could tell back home and he had measured up very well. If you think about it, we took the pressure off him.

8

SITTING ON
GOD'S RIGHT HAND

I WAS UNDER THE MISTAKEN IMPRESSION THAT GENERALS ran the Army; this is not true. The Army is run by a long line of NCOs, which stands for "Non-Commissioned Officers." On the eve of Operation Desert Storm, General Norman Schwarzkopf said, "I have implemented a very good ground war plan. If it goes bad, I'm relying on my NCOs to make it right." He didn't say his "staff officers" and he didn't say his "field officers." He said his NCOs. The NCO rank starts at Corporal and goes up through Specialist Four Buck Sergeant, Specialist Five, Staff Sergeant, Specialist Six, Sergeant First Class, First Sergeant, all the way to Sergeant Major. I've always thought the best rank in the Army was Warrant Officer. All he did was fly the aircraft. He did not command people.

And I still think the best NCO rank is the Specialist Five. I was a Specialist Five; I got paid the same as an E-5 Sergeant but I didn't take command of a large group of soldiers. It's been said a Specialist Five sits at God's right hand. NCOs had a habit of taking things into their own hands. When we moved up to Phubai, we didn't have a bar or a shower house. We gave up our ration cards to the manager of the bar so he could go to the depot and pick up beer and liquor to stock the bar. The ration card regulated how much beer, liquor, and cigarettes you could buy. We also gave up our little Sanyo refrigerators to keep the beer and pop nice and cold.

We built the bar out of old plywood that was borrowed from the Navy; don't ask. We had an old bumper pool table that was donated by the Air Force; don't ask again. It was a very nice arrangement. We got our seed money back in two months.

The showers were a little more difficult. We needed a storage tank and heating coils for warm showers. We "borrowed" a water tank from the Air Force and bartered heating coils from the Navy in exchange for the Air Force bumper pool table. We had warm showers and were the envy of Camp Eagle. The officers were jealous and wanted us to build them a shower house. Of course, we told them to go fuck themselves.

Their response was, "We'll just take yours." And they did. Two nights later, somebody blew it up. So nobody took showers. This went on for about a week, and everyone was getting a little gamey. By the time the no-shower punishment was in its second week, the odor in the barracks was becoming permanent.

I had just come back from the flight line and was sitting in the barracks when it started to rain. The rain was cold and coming down harder by the minute. I couldn't stand it any longer and started stripping off my clothes. I grabbed a bar of soap and ran out into the sidewalk area and started showering. Everyone was yelling at me, "You crazy son-of-a-bitch, you bean pole!" *That's right. At least I'm a clean beanpole.*

The next thing I knew, there were eighty guys taking a shower with me. The Inspector General was driving by and saw half the company taking a shower outside. Oh yeah, I forgot— there was also a reporter with him. The next day, the water was turned back on, the showers were fixed, and life was good again—or as good as life could be in Vietnam. They just didn't want to see a six-foot-seven beanpole with a boney ass taking a shower outside anymore.

I found out very quickly that if you wanted some of the creature comforts that were denied you by the war you had to earn them, buy them, or steal them—and not necessarily in that order. I think my Methodist mother would be appalled.

9

LADIES OF THE NIGHT

I T WAS NO SECRET THAT THE TOWN OF PLEIKU was owned by the American forces by day and by the Viet Cong at night. I thought it was a little odd that this arrangement had gone on for a long time. Then I figured that the soldiers were the economic aid the town needed to survive, the cash infusion as it were.

You could go to town and get yourself a "steam and cream," as we called it. You could take the bus to town and relax in the steam room and then get a full massage. Usually a young Vietnamese girl would give you a full massage, walk on your back, and then she would turn you over and give you a happy ending.

This was going to be my main objective of the day. I had been looking forward to a nice, hot steam bath and a full body massage. I decided to duck into this bar and have one blast and then continue on to the massage parlor. I sat at the bar and ordered a bourbon and water.

Out of the corner of my eye, I caught a glimpse of a tall,

French-Vietnamese girl. She was wearing heels and a miniskirt. She was smartly dressed and a natural beauty. She would walk past me and make snide remarks like, "You so young, does your mother know you're here? This is a place for men, not cherry boys like you." She was trying to get me to tell her to come over and then she would ask me to buy her a Saigon tea.

I had this baby face and everyone thought I was a cherry boy. So I decided to play along; this would be fun. I asked her what her name was. She said it was Lynn.

I said, "Every Vietnamese girl is named Lynn."

"I only sit down with men; not boys who look like babies," she said.

"Maybe you could educate me in the finer aspects of becoming a man."

"What are you saying, cherry boy?"

"Well," I said, "you could help me become a man."

"First you have to buy me Saigon tea and then we will talk."

I knew this ploy. It was the oldest game in history. I kept buying her tea with no alcohol and I kept drinking alcohol, spending more and more money.

I told her flat out, "Wouldn't you rather I give you the money for boom-boom than give it to the bar owner for watered-down drinks?" She agreed and told me to leave and that she would meet me down the street. We met and she led me to a place we called "Shanty Town."

Shanty Town was made up of small, cube-like buildings made out of corrugated tin with tin roofs. Inside this one there was a linoleum floor over hard dirt. There was a small bed as the main piece of furniture, with an orange crate for a night stand.

I had to duck to get in the door but that was OK, because I figured I'd be in a different position soon. We soon got down to business. It was all I expected it to be and more.

That's when she said, "You no cherry boy, you done this before."
I told her, "I never said I was a cherry boy. You said I was a
cherry boy."

I was not watching the time go by and it was getting late. We
both fell asleep and didn't wake up till ten o'clock at night. I was
trapped in Shanty Town with a French-Vietnamese Madame K
surrounded by the Viet Cong.

We heard voices for the next couple hours and she translated
their conversations for me. There was no indication they, the Viet
Cong, were looking for me. Inside I was hoping the MPs *were*
looking for me, but nobody knew I was gone. They would figure
it out by the six o'clock formation, however. This girl could have
given me up, but she didn't. In order to keep her quiet I kept
paying for more sex. We'd have sex, then fall asleep.

I cursed the predicament I was in. I had made a bad judgment
call. I had been thinking with the head below my waist instead
of the one above my shoulders. I figured I could keep this up until
about five o'clock in the morning, as long as the money held out.
If the Viet Cong caught me, they would either kill me or torture
me or both.

When we both had to use the outside bathroom about fifty
yards away, we decided to pee into a coffee can. I woke up at
about five o'clock and looked outside; everything seemed quiet.
We both got dressed and quietly crept out of Shanty Town. Here
was this six-foot-seven aviator being led by a five-foot-four
French-Vietnamese girl. She led me out of Shanty Town to the
main road to Camp Holloway. A lambretta bus was coming down
the road, so we flagged it down.

Before I got on the bus she grabbed my arm and said, "Maybe
you come see me tomorrow and bring more money."

I looked at her and smiled and said, "Oh yeah, I'll be back." I
chased down the lambretta bus and negotiated with the driver.

In the back of the bus were six hooch maids going to Camp Holloway. The bus pulled up to the main gate and the hooch maids got out. I knew I wasn't gonna pass for a hooch maid, so I nonchalantly walked past the guard, showing my ID. He stopped me, asking me where I was coming from.

Just then a friend of mine showed up and told the guard he would handle this. He spoke on my behalf. We had met in Basic Training. After that he had gone to MP school, and I had gone to aviation school.

He said, "Tommy, what the fuck are you doing? What's going on?"

I decided that the truth would be the best way to go here. I said, "I spent the whole night with a prostitute because I missed the bus."

He said, "You're aware the Viet Cong own the town at night?" I said I knew that. He said, "You fucking lucky bastard, you could have been killed."

I said, "I know, I know. If I don't make this next formation everyone's gonna know."

"Get out of here, get to your company, and you owe me one, you fucker."

"OK. I got some Jim Beam," I said, "stop by my hooch and we'll have one."

He yelled, "It's gonna cost more than that! What was the name of the prostitute?"

I yelled back, "Lynn!"

"They're all named Lynn!"

I took off running to the company area.

The morning formation was assembling and the roll call was being taken. I just got to my normal position when the Platoon Sergeant called my name.

I said, "Here, Sarge."

He looked at me and said, "You're flying standby, so get into your nomex flight suit."

I said, "Right away, Sarge," and left.

I got to the aircraft and performed a preflight inspection. Then I lay down, took a nap, and thought to myself, *I beat the devil and got away with it. I'm never gonna make that mistake again.* I never told anybody about this narrow escape because it was stupid and careless. It was not like me, to make an error in judgment like that. Vietnam, Cambodia, and Laos were dangerous countries, and I had better be at my best.

DEALS WE
MAKE WITH GOD

I F YOU FLY LONG ENOUGH, OR IF YOU'RE A SOLDIER in the field,
it's possible to get into many close calls or tight situations. At
times, things could seem pretty hopeless. There's an old saying:
"There are no atheists in foxholes." It was certainly true. Nobody
liked to talk about it, but it was true. Whenever we got into
trouble we called on The Almighty. One example was: "God, you
get me out of this and I'll go to church a whole month of
Sundays." My favorite was: "God, you get me out of this and I'll
go to confession." Oh yeah, God wanted to hear your confession
so you could do it all over again next week.

I have to say, I was no different, but I hated doing it because it
seemed so hypocritical. The chaplain would stop around your
hooch and check to see if things were alright. Sometimes he
would engage us in a game of horseshoes or basketball. He was
generally our friend and took a real, honest interest in us. He
would always stop by my hooch because I was a Methodist and

so was he, but he could do a Baptist service or any other
Protestant service. He couldn't do Jewish or Catholic services,
though.

The flight platoon guys were a bunch of crazy bastards, but that
chaplain was not afraid of us. He would walk right into the lion's
den. I respected him for that. We would have some really good
arguments. He knew I made deals with God. He didn't like it one
bit, but he understood why we did it. The whole time I was in
Vietnam, I got good at praying. I just wasn't real showy about it. I
figured it was between me and God. They say God protects morons
and idiots, and I'm pretty sure I qualified for his protection.

II

NIGHT MOVES

ONE OF THE MOST HAZARDOUS DUTIES YOU COULD HAVE was being stationed at a firebase. The firebase was usually perched up on a hill or a mountain. There were typically four or five artillery pieces, such as 105 howitzers, field cannons, or 155 howitzers, on these positions. Firebases were positioned so they could cover one another's flanks and kill zones, and were somewhat vulnerable at night. That's where we came in.

Night vision goggles were just starting to come into their own, and were relatively new, clumsy and not that readily available. So, the idea was for a Chinook to fly around the firebase at about three thousand feet, dropping these large canister flares. The trap door on the bottom belly of the Chinook was rigged with a chute so you could set the flare to go off at a certain altitude. Then you hooked up a lanyard to pull out the flare parachute. If everything worked correctly, the flare fell out of the aircraft, the lanyard pulled out the parachute, and a few seconds later, the flare ignited and lit up the perimeter of the firebase with one million candlelight of brightness.

When these flares went off, it almost looked like daytime. If the enemy was spotted, artillery was called in or a gunship came in and laid down fire with rockets or mini guns. The problem with flares was, if the wind shifted and blew the flare over the firebase, the firebase was lit up and then the enemy knew where we were. The other problem was that the flare might ignite too close to the Chinook, giving away our position exactly. The flares had a nice, twelve-foot diameter parachute on them and stayed in the air a long time.

I never liked these missions because we usually carried twelve thousand pounds of fuel. If a flare ignited too close to the ship, God knows what could have happened. When you looked down and got too close, you could see the flares falling slowly to earth, exposing the enemy positions.

Firebases were set up all along the Ho Chi Minh Trail, which was the main supply route of the NVA. The theory behind this was that putting a firebase every two to three miles would disrupt NVA supplies and reinforcements. The 179th was the only inland assault support helicopter company, so therefore we covered all the mountain territories along the Cambodian and Laotian borders.

In order to do these missions, we had to be outfitted with more powerful engines. Gradually the Army brought in the more powerful Super C Chinooks. We could fly over the mountains and pick up heavier loads. We got pretty good at dropping flares on the enemy positions, but you didn't want to get too close because they'd forget about the firebase and turn their attention on you. That happened quite often.

I noticed that the parachutes on the bigger flares were about twenty-four feet in diameter. So if you put two together, you would have forty-eight feet of canopy to shade you from the sun when you were having cocktails at the bar we had built. These parachutes were very stylish, but very hard to come by. One day we flew into Khe Sahn to refuel. We shut down the aircraft and decided to have C-rations for lunch.

A crew chief from another aircraft came running over to me and said, "I saw a large parachute hung up in some barbed wire fencing." My crew went running over to take a look at the parachute. I stayed back to tell the pilots where we were going. Then I ran to where the other guys were. This crew chief, Jack Mansky, was in the middle of a field. I hopped the fence and took a step, but I didn't like the way the ground felt. I stopped in my tracks and backed out the same way I had come in and hopped the fence to get out.

I said to DJ, "Did you notice anything weird about the ground?"

He replied, "No, why?"

I said, "It's too soft and there's no grass or weeds growing on the ground."

By then, Mansky was at the next fence, near the parachute. He said, "There's a little sign on the fence in red lettering."

DJ turned to me and said in that long drawl of a Texas accent, "I betcha this is a mine field."

Just then Mansky said, "The sign says MINES!"

I said in my Chicago accent, "Son-of-a-bitch, it's a fucking mine field!" As my voice was going up another octave, I told him, "Stay calm and just walk out the same way you walked in. Or we could get a helicopter, hover, and pick you up. Or we could notify the command and get a blueprint of the mine field."

He said, "I'm walking out of here."

I said, "Are you sure?"

"I'm sure," he said. "If they find out I'll get busted down to private."

He reached for the parachute and I told him, "Just leave that parachute."

He said, "No way, I came this far." He started walking out of the mine field, slowly looking for his old foot prints. DJ and I waited by the fence, sweating our balls off.

DJ told Mansky, "If you put your foot down and you hear a click, just stop right away." DJ said he had seen that on an episode of the television show *Combat.*

I said to DJ, "Well, what happened next?"

He said, "I don't know; I went to the refrigerator to get a cold drink." I looked at him in bewilderment. He said, "I'm sorry, I was thirsty."

I looked at Mansky and said, "If you hear a click, just freeze and we'll go get somebody."

He looked at me and said, "How far am I from the fence?" I told him at least ten yards. He said, "Yep, that's what I figured. I'm gonna run for it and I'm gonna fly over that fence, so you guys better catch me." We tried to tell him no way, but he was already running as hard as he could. He came flying over that fence and we caught him and all fell to the ground. DJ was cursing us out.

This was the dumbest thing that big Yankee had ever done. I turned to DJ. "Oh yeah, you went to the refrigerator for a cold drink when *Combat* was on."

DJ said, "Oh, you gonna try and put this on me now?"

We went back to our Chinooks and never said a word to anyone.

We hung the canopy outside the bar and had a drink to toast the new cover over our patio. For forty-three years the three of us kept that secret. You see, God really did look after morons and idiots. From then on whenever DJ thought about going to the refrigerator for a cold drink, he always waited for the commercial.

12

BACK TO THE
KINGDOM OF LAOS

O PERATIONS WERE STARTING UP AGAIN IN LAOS. Firebases along the Laotian border needed to be resupplied, and our working days were getting longer and longer. We were sometimes flying sixteen-hour days. The pilots were switched out after eight hours, but not the flight crews. The enlisted flight crews stayed on as long as the aircraft was being flown.

I started getting ringing in my ears again and really bad fatigue from lack of sleep. This was going to be the 179th's last campaign into Laos. The rumor mill had us standing down at the end of August and transferring to Fort Carson, Colorado; but that was three months away. There was one more campaign to finish, and that was the evacuation of all the ARVN troops still in Laos.

I started to believe I would get out of Vietnam alive and so wore my chicken plate on every mission, just to help that notion along. I found extra armor plate and laid it down on the floor of the Chinook near the trap door for the hook. I cleaned my M-16 every day. I taped three magazines together so I would have enough fire power. Guys were trying to buy my M-79 grenade launcher; I wasn't going to sell that until the last day of the last mission.

I would have little talks with myself; I thought this behavior was quite unusual, but that didn't stop me from doing it. Deep down inside, you know these fears are blown out of proportion. So what do you do? The answer is, you suffer in silence. You drink beer or whiskey. You keep busy doing your job and doing it well, almost to a fault.

****

One day we were flying along the DMZ with a sling load of 105 ammo, heading for Firebase Alpha, when the pilots notified us that the clouds were getting lower and we had to reduce our altitude.

This meant I had to start watching the load so we wouldn't hit any mountain tops. We had to maintain our airspeed because if we slowed we would be sitting ducks for small arms fire.

I laid down by the trapdoor over the armor plate. The pilots notified me that the firebase was in sight. I was telling the pilots, "Load is fifty off the ground, forty off the ground, thirty off the ground, ten off the ground, four off the ground...." Once the load was on the ground, I released the load and told the pilot to bring the aircraft up and cleared him for flight.

As we pulled up, we banked left and picked up speed, heading for higher altitude. We were suddenly hit by small arms fire. Two rounds came up through the floor of the helicopter; one round hit the armor plate beneath me and the other ricocheted off my helmet. The force of the round hitting my helmet threw me backwards on my ass. I was dazed and confused for a while. The gunners opened up, using up about one thousand rounds of ammo. DJ came running over to me. I took my helmet off and he checked out my head.

He was running his hand through my hair and kept saying. "Nothing, nothing, not a scratch, you lucky motherfucker." I realized I was a lucky motherfucker. I was pretty quiet the rest of the day.

We landed back at base camp. I closed up the ship, went back to my room, and had a few drinks. DJ brought me sandwiches from the mess hall.

A couple of fellow flight engineers came into my room and said, "We heard you almost got your head blown off. Let's party."

I said, "Let's not." Then they became the friends I knew they were. We talked about mojo and karma and luck. It seemed my luck was running out, my karma was bad, and my mojo wasn't working.

The next morning, I went to the dispensary to see about more pills for my dysentery and to see what they could do about the ringing in my ears. The flight surgeon gave me more pills and checked out my ears. He told me everything looked OK and there wasn't anything he could give me for the ringing in my ears.

The flight surgeon then asked, "Is there anything else?"

I replied, "No, see you later."

He stopped me and said, "I heard about your close call."

"Bad news travels fast."

He looked at me and said, "You have a confidence problem and you're getting short." He meant that my time in-country was getting to be less and less.

The next day we were right back in Laos, supplying the same firebases where we had been ambushed. The best way to handle the situation was to get mean and nasty, and stay that way. I told the gunners that if we took small arms fire, they answered with one thousand rounds of ammo, smoke grenades, and regular grenades. I wanted to rain hell on that jungle and tear it up. I didn't give a fuck. If it moved, kill it. This was the new mood I was in. I was on edge and I stayed that way for long time. I think I would have been in a better position if I had gotten to take the first shot instead of reacting to what the enemy was doing. This was the new me for the next three months: a little mean, a little nasty, and ever vigilant. I was double checking all the work I did on the helicopter and double checking everybody else's work too.

****

The Old Man, as we referred to the company commander, was an old-time aviator and ran everything by the book—a loose book. His name was Major Jim Harris. He decided one day that the morale of the company was in a sad state, and he thought a company party would perk us up.

He ordered barbecue pits brought in and a trailer of ice filled with beer. He instructed the mess hall to make up batches of potato salad, pork and beans, and large bowls of salad.

He ordered the NCOs to set up horseshoe, volleyball, and basketball courts. There would be tournaments for everyone on these courts. The tournaments would run all day and night. The bar would keep track of the tournaments and supply the judges.

The main course was going to be T-bone steak. I was not a big fan of steak, because my mother would cook round steak for us as kids. The round steak tasted like shoe leather still on the shoe. I was not going to eat any steak, but my friends insisted this was *T-bone steak*. They said this was a tender cut of prime steak and I would love it. So I loaded up my plate with potato salad, beans, cottage cheese, regular salad, and a nice, juicy T-bone.

I cut into that steak and I already knew this was a different cut of meat, just by the way the knife moved through it. When you cut round steak the way my mother made it, the knife labors through the meat, struggling to make its mark. This meat surrendered itself to the knife and parted from the rest of the meat easily. I put the first piece in my mouth and the juices from that bite gently flowed into my mouth. *Oh yes. This is such a heavenly experience!*

I ate the whole steak, along with everything else on my plate. My morale was getting better already. I told the Old Man that if I could have another steak I would be downright giddy. He responded with a polite, "No, one per person."

I said, "That's OK, there's horseshoes to play and some drinking to catch up on." From that day on, I've never had a piece of round steak. After all, my body is a temple and I should treat it as such.

I wandered over to the horseshoe pits and played a little. This was really not my game, but I could kind of bluff my way through. Now, basketball—there was my game, and I quickly got into a game of NCOs against officers. It started out friendly, but turned into the biggest hack game I ever saw. The NCOs won the game by one point. Tempers flared and there was a lot of pushing and shoving. Talk about trash talk; I think my mother was mentioned two or three times over the course of the game.

Officers are supposed to be gentlemen. Ha and double ha! In order to beat them, we had to get nastier than they were. We were drawing a large crowd. There was more yelling and screaming. This was like a college game. I was considered a fair player and always played by the rules. But in this game, all bets were off. I was getting elbowed and pushed around, so I resorted to guerilla basketball. I can also trash talk with the best of them.

I told one officer I was gonna beat him like a red-headed step child, sir. As I've already mentioned, you have to say "sir" at the beginning or the end of a sentence. Something like this: "Sir, your girlfriend is so fat she could jump into Lake Michigan and when she got out of the lake, she would leave a ring around the shore, sir." Kind of takes the sting out of trash talk. "Sir, you're from the South, is that right? Did you go to the same college as Opie Taylor, sir?"

The game was over and the trash talk was still going on. Finally the Old Man had had enough and said, "Let's stop this bullshit before it gets out of hand." This one game could have ruined the whole day, but the Old Man was too smart for that to happen. We parted shaking hands, not apologizing, but we did have to work together. After that, there were no more officers playing against NCOs. We usually split the sides up and everyone was happy.

The Old Man would sometimes come down to the basketball court and play a little one-on-one or two-on-two. We never roughed him up, but he could take a good shot. We respected the hell out of him. He wasn't an armchair commander. He could fly Chinooks with the best of them. He pulled some of the worst missions right beside us. He led from the front and we respected that. Three things came out of that company party: my morale improved, I had a new respect for the company commander and his officers, and I discovered a new cut of steak called T-bone.

13

A DIFFERENT
KIND OF ENEMY

I F A PSYCHIATRIST WANTED TO GET INTO A COMBAT veteran's head he would have a hard time, because there is no room in there. A combat veteran has too much to think about. He is always on alert and vigilant. At least, that's the way it should be. Sadly, however, this is usually not the case. The most important thing he thinks about is his girlfriend or wife. When is the next letter coming? Why isn't she writing? What's taking so long for the mail to get here? The worst is the dreaded "Dear John" letter. If women only understood what happened in Vietnam when a guy got a "Dear John" letter. I have seen the most cool, calm, collected guys go ballistic over a girlfriend or wife after one of these letters. To take the pressure off, the Army sent the married guys to Hawaii to meet their wives for R&R.

I didn't have this problem because I had cut the cord before I came to Vietnam. So I was a free agent, so to speak. I wrote to other women; my sisters don't count. I think a combat vet could put up with just about anything if everything was all right at home. If things weren't right at home, you had one unhappy G.I., and maybe a crazy one. I know I got a little angry myself, and the letters weren't even from my girl.

The absolute worst was the divorce. It went something like this: "I'm divorcing you and marrying your best friend and taking the kids and the dog." We seriously considered taking up a collection and hiring a hit man to solve the problem. Cooler heads always prevailed. No telling what happened when he got home. Sometimes I thought the wife waited till he was gone to start pulling all this shit. She counted on him not coming home for a long time.

Oh yes, here's my favorite: A guy was in Vietnam for six months. He got a letter from his wife that said she was four months pregnant and insisted the baby was his. This was the letter you threw darts at. With all these distractions, it was a wonder a combat soldier was ever able to focus on his duties.

The most dangerous enemy was the unseen one that was never talked about: drugs and alcohol abuse. I rarely talked about this topic, because it destroyed too many of my friends while serving in Vietnam. I feared I would go to the dark side and never come back, feared I would enter their world and stay there for good.

I had two friends taken off flight status and put on menial tasks because the company commander lost confidence in them due to their drug abuse. They were taken from our barracks and put into separate quarters, which we nicknamed the "head shed." It was common knowledge that my two friends were snorting heroin, otherwise called "bitch." It was so bad that they couldn't have a decent bowel movement.

One night I walked into the latrine to do my nightly squeeze and read the latest issue of *Playboy* magazine. To my surprise, I startled my two druggy friends, who were bent over the toilets with their fingers up their rectums. At first I thought this was some kind of perverted homosexual activity.

I immediately asked these guys, "What the fuck are you doing?" They said they couldn't take a regular shit anymore, so they were trying to reach up and pull the turds out.

I told them if they were homosexuals I would accept it. But turd pulling, I don't think so. This was not normal. They assured me they were not homosexuals.

"Well if you are, just don't hit on me," I said. I told them to go to the dispensary to get an enema, or a "torpedo," to shove up their yoo-hoo and everything would be fine. They protested that the dispensary asked too many questions and they might think they were drug addicts.

I immediately responded, "But you are drug addicts!" I knew I was out of my league here. I was not very knowledgeable about drug abuse. I was preaching and advising these two guys to quit the drug and get straight, but to no avail. I knew if they didn't quit soon, they wouldn't be getting out of Vietnam.

That night I went back to my hooch and poured myself a Jim Beam and 7Up and thought about my friends' problem. I suddenly realized I had a drug in my hand. I poured it down my mouth and they snorted theirs up their noses. I was no better than they were, except I could move my bowels, and my drug was socially acceptable.

****

Just when I thought things couldn't get any worse, they did. I went to mail call the next afternoon and I received three letters from home, but one of them actually wasn't from home. I opened the strange letter from a girl from the New England area. As it turned out, she was the girlfriend of Jack Mansky, one of the guys hooked on heroin. When I saw who had written it, I stuffed the letter into my shirt and ran back to the barracks.

The whole time I was running to the barracks I was wondering, *Why is she writing to me?* I was hoping she didn't want to get romantically involved with me, because that would get your ass shot off faster than anything. *How did she get my name? Why was she writing me?* I started reading the letter. She introduced herself as Jack Mansky's girlfriend, and said she was worried about Jack because his letters lately didn't make sense. She was wondering if he was taking drugs and wanted me to confirm that he was.

For the next thirty minutes, I was angry at her for putting me in this position and angry at Jack for doing heroin and getting kicked off flight status. His jobs now included picking up trash in the company area and supervising the shit burner. I folded the letter back up neatly and threw it to the back of my locker, padlocked the door, and tried not to think about what I was going to do.

I decided it was time to get back to what I did best, and that was being a flight engineer on a CH-47 Chinook. My days as drug counselor were over. My ship had been in depot maintenance for a week. All the transmissions had been replaced and some new rotors had been installed. The test pilots flew her a couple of times, and we were ready to go. The crew reinstalled the sound proofing, floor plates, and armor plating. Finally, we installed the gun mounts for the M-60 machine guns and we were ready to go.

The very next day, we were assigned a mission. I was awakened at 5:00 a.m., got dressed, and put on my flight suit and my leather boots. I opened up my locker and there, staring at me, was the infernal, troublemaking letter. I ran scenarios in my head on how I would approach Jack with this dilemma.

"Hey Jack, I got a letter from your girl yesterday."

His reply would be, "Why is she writing to you?"

"Well Jack, she suspects you're on drugs and wants me to confirm it."

His response would be, "Well just write her back and tell her I'm not on drugs."

My response would be, "I could do that, Jack, but that would be a lie, and that wouldn't help you."

This could get very ugly, very fast. After all, we all have guns and we all know how to use them. Once again I folded the letter up and threw it to the back of my locker. This was so like me to do this. I procrastinated like you wouldn't believe. Jack would always show her picture around to everyone. He would say, "Look what's waiting for me when I get home." I would agree she was a very pretty girl and he was a very lucky fellow.

Then I wondered, *How the hell did she get my name?* He had probably written her and told her he had a friend who was tall and fairly good-looking who needed a pen pal. I was a free agent and I liked it. These other guys had wives and girlfriends, which made them wacky. Me, I had Jim Beam and Madame Ks. If worst came to worst, I could always sneak back into town and see Lynn. Or I could get shot in the ass and spend the next two-and-a-half months on a hospital ship. But sadly, I had no ass. All I had were two hamburger buns glued to my hips. It would take a real sharpshooter to hit this ass. I thought, Oh, fuck it, and closed my locker, picked up my flight gear, and started walking to the flight line.

DJ, my crew chief, caught up with me. I said, "Where's Kenny, the left gunner?"

He said, "He had to go to the dentist." I noticed a young boy tagging behind us. I looked at him. He still had pimples on his face. The kid was looking for the crew of 18528.

DJ told him, "Well, you found us."

The kid replied, "Great; I'm your new gunner." We stopped dead in our tracks.

DJ looked at the boy and said, "Boy, you don't even shave, do you?"

The boy answered nervously, "Sometimes I do."

"Next time you shave," DJ said, "put some cream on your face and let the cat lick it off."

I thought this was very amusing and I asked the boy, "Where are you from?" He said he had citizenship in both Canada and the United States. I asked if we were running out of Americans to fight this war.

"We don't have our own war to fight so I thought I'd come help you guys fight this one."

"Thank you very kindly," I said. "We need all the help we can get."

Then he asked if we knew the flight engineer on 18528. "I heard he was a real dick." With that, DJ started to crack up and pointed to me. This kid looked at me and said, "Oh, I guess you're the flight engineer."

"That's me. Mr. Dickhead to you."

We got to the aircraft. The kid tried to recover from his blunder by saying, "This ship is a real beauty. Maybe we'll see some action today."

I responded, "You're gonna see some action right now."

He said, "Really?"

"Really. Go get two M-60 machine guns, five thousand rounds of ammo, clean the pilot's windshield, sweep the floors on the ship, go get fifty feet of flight line and one bucket of prop wash and two cans of compression."

The kid ran off to find everything. He had excitement and a lot of energy. DJ came over to me and said, "There's no such thing as a can of compression."

I said, "I know, and prop wash is the wind caused by the movement of the rotors."

"Flight line is where you park the aircraft," DJ said.

"I know."

DJ smirked and asked, "How long are you gonna keep this up?"

"Till he really does have to shave."

"You really are a dickhead."

Yes, I was, but I really liked the kid. He had energy, opinions, and said what was on his mind. Kinda reminded me of somebody.

****

DJ was growing tired of all the shit and thought if he got shot in the leg, he could spend the rest of his tour on a hospital ship, lounging around. I told him it wasn't his turn to get shot; it was my turn.

He said, "Oh, that's bullshit; you got shot two weeks ago."

I told him, "That doesn't count. The bullet ricocheted off my helmet. I never got hurt. No blood was drawn, so it's still my turn."

DJ looked at me in disgust and said, "You really are a dickhead. I really had plans on resting on a hospital ship." This kind of banter went on and on.

Just then the pilots came on board and we started the preflight inspection. When the pilots finished the inspection, we were ready to go. The pilots took one look at the new gunner and asked me if this kid was old enough.

One pilot said, "He looks so young, he looks like the pizza delivery boy back home."

I told him, "Back home would be Canada."

The pilot replied, "He's from Canada?"

"Yes, sir, he is."

"Well, Chief, are we running out of American boys?"

"Apparently we are, sir. You see, sir, Canada doesn't have a war so he decided to join ours."

The banter continued. It was meant to ease the tension. We closed up the cowling and put on our helmets. The pilots went through a checklist; we connected to the intercom and radios. The following is the start-up sequence for a CH-47 Chinook:

The pilot states: "Ready on the 'P,'" short for "APU," which stands for Auxiliary Power Unit. This is a small turbine engine that powers the generators and all hydraulic systems. The APU will start the larger number #1 and #2 engines when ready. The flight engineer will reply, "Ready on the 'P.'" If everything is OK, the pilots will go on to the next step.

The pilot states: "Ready on #1." This is the engine on the left side of the aircraft, looking from the rear of the aircraft. The flight engineer is positioned near the #1 engine with a fire extinguisher. If everything is OK he says, "Ready on #1 engine." The pilot starts the #1 engine. Slowly the engine turns over, ignites, and the blades start turning. The front blades turn in a counter-clockwise direction, and the rear blades turn in a clockwise direction. The aircraft looks like it's doing a hula dance. At this time, the pilots go through another checklist.

The pilot states: "Ready on #2." If everything looks good, the flight engineer replies, "Ready on #2 engine." The pilot starts the #2 engine. They go through another checklist. If everything is alright, they bring the aircraft to proper rotor speed.

The pilot requests permission to taxi from the tower. If the tower gives permission, the flight engineer kicks the chocks out and puts them in the aircraft. The chocks prevent the aircraft from rolling. The flight engineer hops into the aircraft and raises the ramp and tells the pilots, "Ramps up, ready in the rear."

These two pilots were very young, but very good; they were known to be "hot dogs." They should have been in a steamed bun with a dab of mustard. That was OK, I liked hot dogs. The worst thing you could do to me was bore me to death; these two were not boring.

We taxied off the flight line, out to the main taxiway. Normal pilots would go onto the runway and lift up vertically in the air and start their assent to the desired altitude. Not these two; they wanted to take off like a normal, fixed-wing aircraft. When they did this, the helicopter got rolling very fast. The front wheels came off the ground about two feet and the rear wheels stayed on the ground till you got to the end of the runway, pulled thrust, and gained altitude. Everyone liked this takeoff. It felt cool and it looked cool.

I looked over at the new kid. He had a broad smile on his face. I thought he was going to wet his pants, he was so excited. He leaned over to talk to me.

"Hey, Chief, maybe we'll see some action."

"Maybe," I said, though I really would rather have settled for a nice milk run. DJ and I were running on pure experience. We had run out of karma and mojo and luck a long time ago.

The pilots informed us we would be flying along the Laotian border, looking for a downed Huey gunship. A security team had been sent in to set up a perimeter, and a rigging team was already there to install the lifting straps so the Huey could be picked up by the Chinook.

The Huey guys would just cringe whenever one of their aircraft was picked up by a Chinook. They were under the impression that the Huey was a better aircraft than the Chinook, but it was slower and less powerful. We used to whiz by these guys so fast, we would flip them the bird as we flew by. We would go to their bar and tell them, "Hey listen, today we picked your Huey up out of the jungle, again." This would really piss them off.

The pathfinders gave us the coordinates and the pilots decided to make their final approach coming out of the sun. That way, enemy snipers couldn't see us till the last minute. I opened the trap door to the cargo hook and set the hook in place. If everything went well, we would be over the downed Huey in less than thirty seconds.

We came out of the sun at about 130 knots. The pilots brought the Chinook over the Huey and I took control of the directions and guided them down. The hook-up guy was experienced and slammed the rigging donut on the hook, quickly getting out of the way. I ordered the pilots to climb and cleared them for takeoff. The Huey slowly came off the ground. As we started gaining altitude, the gunners caught a small arm muzzle flash and immediately started putting down suppressing fire on the area of the muzzle flash. We caught the enemy in an open clearing in the jungle. The kid fired about five hundred rounds and really tore up the area.

I leaped from my station and threw out a smoke grenade. I caught a glimpse of an NVA soldier twitching and convulsing. He had been hit by M-60 rounds. The cobra gunships came in and mopped up the area with their mini guns. We took the downed Huey back to Camp Eagle and dropped it ever so softly in the maintenance area. We landed at the 179th flight line. The pilots shut down the engines.

We checked out the ship for more bullet holes, but we couldn't find any. I found out later that they were shooting at the Huey as we were hauling it away. I was feeling pretty good. I had a grin on my face like a Cheshire cat. I couldn't wait to go to the bar where the Huey guys hung out and tell them we had hauled another Huey out of the jungle.

I looked at the new gunner and he looked a little depressed. I said, "What's wrong with you?"

"Didn't you see the way that NVA soldier convulsed and twitched when I shot him?"

"I did see him," I said. "What did you expect? That's what a 7.62 mm round does. Especially when you keep firing at the same guy. You fired way too many rounds." This was expected from an inexperienced gunner. "You fired so many rounds, you may have warped the barrel. What was your name?"

"Coley Van Kamppen, from Canada."

"Well, Coley Van Kamppen from Canada, the pilots are safe, DJ is fine, I'm fine, you're fine, and the ship is fine."

"I don't feel fine. In fact, I feel like throwing up."

"Don't throw up here, you have to sweep the floor of the aircraft and clean the guns and return them to the armory."

"I didn't think it would be like this."

"Hey kid, this ain't the movies. After you shoot somebody he doesn't get up to do the next scene. Forget that Hollywood shit; that ain't real. This is real. Look, why don't you go on the other side of the revetment, throw up, and go back to the barracks. DJ and I can take care of the guns."

He looked at me with a little agitation and said, "I can do my job." He picked up the guns and ammo and started walking to the armory, throwing up the whole way.

DJ said, "I never saw a guy throw up so much all over the flight line."

"I know, don't step in it and track it back on board."

"Hope it rains tonight, 'cause I ain't cleaning it up."

"I betcha he wishes he was back in Canada, delivering pizzas."

"Let's go get supper. All that evacuation made me hungry."

We waited for the kid and asked if he was alright.

"No, I feel like shit."

"We're going to the mess hall if you want to come."

"No, I think I'll go back to the barracks and rest."

In my best Father Flannigan voice I said, "You need to eat some fruit, like apples or bananas, my son."

"You guys always like this?"

"Like what?"

"Like being dickheads all the time."

"Yeah, pretty much. Maybe we should give you a sugar titty."

"What's that?"

"We take a wash cloth, wet it, dip it in sugar, and let you suck on it."

"You forget that I want the real thing."

"Now you're talking; the day after tomorrow we are all going to town."

"What's in town?"

I answered, "Steam and cream, buddy boy, steam and cream. You go to a massage parlor, get a good steam, then a good massage, and then you get a happy ending."

"What's a happy ending?"

"Don't worry, you'll figure it out."

I went back to my hooch and opened my locker. The letter was still there. Nobody had stolen it. I thought to myself, *This girl is really smart, much too smart for Jack Mansky. If a marriage was going to come out of this union, she would have to take the lead.* Once again, I folded the letter up and threw it back into my locker.

I was going by the mess hall to get some ice for my beverages. I passed by the bulletin board and noticed a new flyer. This flyer was announcing a new program for the fight on drugs. A drug addict would have to admit he was a drug addict and submit to both a urinalysis test and to a thirty-day detoxification program. He could enter the program two months before his time was up in Vietnam. If he completed the program, he could get an honorable discharge.

I read the flyer twice looking for loopholes, the same thing lawyers do when they're reading the law. I studied it and thought it might be an answer to a big problem. I decided to think about it for a while. Once again, I was the great procrastinator. The next day was Thursday; steam and cream day. We headed to downtown Pleiku. We hitched a ride in a supply truck. I saw the club where I had met the French-Vietnamese girl. I told the guys I would catch up with them later on. I walked into a bar called the Hollywood Bar and Grill. What a stretch. I went over to the bar and ordered a Jim Beam and water.

I asked the man behind the bar, "Are you the owner?" He nodded his head.

"So, where is Lynn?"

"She go to doctor today. Who are you?"

"What's wrong with her? My name is Tom."

"I think she pregnant."

"How do you know that?"

"She has the morning sickness. She throw up."

"Could be something else."

"Nah, I hired her to be waitress, but she doing Madame K on the side."

"Well, I have to go."

"What your last name, Tom?"

"Jefferson, Thomas Jefferson."

"I tell her you looking for her."

I walked out of the bar feeling I had dodged a bullet. I walked across the street and noticed a bunch of cowboys playing with another Madame K, sort of pushing her around. It was no secret that I hated the fuckers. I'd rather put a bullet in these guys than the NVA. I ignored them and walked into the steam room. I took off my clothes and wrapped a towel around my waist, sat down on a wooden bench, and soaked in the steam for the next half hour.

After the steam I was put on a massage table and given a good workout. She cupped her hand and slowly beat my back, making a glucking noise with her hands. I turned over and looked at her face. She had a cute face, but it was marred by black and blue marks around her left eye.

I said, "Nice shiner. Who gave you that?"

"Cowboys. They number hucking ten." (Vietnamese had a tough time pronouncing Fs.)

"Why did they hit you?"

"I owe money for protection."

After the massage, I went outside and found DJ. After I told him what the cowboys had done to that poor girl, he looked at me and said, "What poor excuses for human beings." I agreed.

I told DJ my dad had bought me this beautiful pocket knife before I left for Vietnam. He had sharpened it till it was razor-thin sharp. My dad had said it might come in handy someday. DJ and I walked along the long row of motorcycles the cowboys had parked in front of the bar. We started looking for our ride.

We hailed a three-quarter-ton truck from the 1st Cav and he offered three of us, Coley had now joined DJ and I, a ride back to Camp Holloway. We got into the back of the truck and off we went. Somebody picked up an old beer bottle and threw it at the motorcycles. The cowboys came out of the bar and started chasing us back to Camp Holloway on their motorcycles.

I told the driver, "Hey, Mac, you better step on it. Cowboys are chasing us."

"I hate cowboys."

"Don't we all."

The cowboys were catching up to us. We started looking around for something to throw at them. For some reason, their front tires were going flat. The tires were wrapping around the forks and the rims were bending out of shape. They were forced to quit chasing us.

Coley said, "What are the odds that ten motorcycles would have ten flat tires?"

DJ looked at him and said, "Pretty good odds."

"Well, it doesn't matter. It was a happy ending."

I said, "Speaking of happy endings, did the girl in the massage parlor take care of you?"

"Oh yeah, she was great. In fact, I'm gonna ask her if we can start dating."

DJ and I looked at each other and started laughing.

DJ said, "Maybe you can bring her home to your mother."

"No seriously, she was great. Especially that thing she did with her finger."

"What thing was that?"

I said, "Yeah, what thing was that and what are you talking about?"

"It's too late. You guys lost your chance to find out."

I said, "Maybe we'll start 'dating' her."

DJ said, "Does that cost extra?"

"She said she liked me and kept calling me 'cherry boy.' In fact, I was wondering when we could go back."

"I think you should concentrate on your job and on staying alive."

"But you were the guys who showed me this great experience."

"It's not something you can do every day."

"For six bucks I got a steam, massage, and a happy ending. Why can't I do it every day?"

Well, how could I argue with logic like that? "You're just a Pfc. You don't make enough money to go out whoring every day. We had a great day, we got a steam, massage, a happy ending, and we tangled with some cowboys. Does it get any better than this?"

DJ said, "Yes, it does; the day you go home."

We drove through the gate at Camp Holloway, got out, and

showed the MPs our IDs. My friend the MP asked me if we had
seen any trouble in town with the cowboys.

DJ said, "We don't associate with draft-dodging criminals."

I said, "You heard him."

DJ looked at the kid and said quietly, "Shut up."

The MP looked at me and said, "You still got that bottle of
scotch?"

"Bourbon."

"Same thing."

"No, it's not."

"I'll stop by sometime."

"You better hurry up, because I'm getting short."

I went back to my hooch and started writing letters back home
to my parents and sisters. Not letters that spoke the truth. They
were lighthearted letters, wondering what they were doing, how's
school, the same old pabulum.

I went to my locker, opened it, pulled out the letter from
Mansky's girlfriend, and read it three times. I was looking for a
way out. I was reading between the lines; nothing there. Then I
had a moment of genius. I don't know why I hadn't thought of it
before; it was so simple. I would fold the letter back up neatly,
seal it, and write across the envelope, "Deceased." I was amazed
at myself for coming up with a solution so simple and diabolical.
I poured myself a little 7Up mixed with a little Jim Beam to toast
myself on the success of my brilliancy. I had beaten the cunning
young girl in New England. I was basking in my own glory. I
stopped my celebration when I realized the military would never
say "Deceased." What they would say was, "No longer at this
address," no…"No longer in country, no…"No longer receiving
mail." None of these were any good. The military loved one or
two-word answers. I thought long and hard about this. What
would be the proper nomenclature? The Army loves nomenclature.
Then it came to me: "Not Deliverable." I was back to congratulating

myself. I was feeling so good, I went to the basketball court and engaged in a rousing game of H.O.R.S.E. The weight of the world had been taken off me.

Two days later, Kenny, the regular gunner, was back, minus a tooth. I looked at his mouth.

I said, "There's a huge gap."

He said, "No shit. It hurts like hell when I suck wind. How'd the new gunner work out?"

DJ said, "He did fine. If you can keep him away from the whores, he'll even do better."

"Why, what happened?"

"He went into town with us the other day and got his tubes cleaned out. Now he wants to date one of the girls."

"Did anyone explain to him you don't date prostitutes? Whose idea was it to go to town?" DJ looked at me.

I said, "The kid had a bad day on the gun. He needed to relax. It was his first time and he's from Canada."

"No shit, don't they have prostitutes in Canada?"

"Apparently not; at least, not for six bucks."

"Six bucks? That's high."

"He got a steam, massage, and a really good happy ending."

"What do you mean, a real good happy ending?"

"Go see her and find out."

"No shit, you never took me there. How come you never took me there?"

"Because you're married. I would be leading you astray."

It was time to pull rank and get this aircraft inspected and ready for flight.

"Kenny, it's time to go to work. Get the guns and ammo. Clean the windshield and sweep the aircraft out. DJ, let's get this aircraft ready. Pilots are on their way." I was sounding like a flight engineer, barking out orders. Very seldom did I do this. I usually led by example.

14

PIG IN A BASKET

WE TOOK OFF FROM PLEIKU AND HEADED TO Kontum to work with Special Forces. We were relocating a Montagnard village and bringing it closer to the Special Forces camp. The villagers packed up their belongings and carried them on their backs. The livestock were put into cages made from tree branches and twine. They wove a basket around a large sow, hoping this would hold her for the trip to the camp. When they were all loaded into the Chinook, we took off from the village and everything seemed fine.

The noise from the transmissions and engines was bothering the pig. Montagnards tried to calm the pig by rubbing its ears and head. The pig was struggling to get out of the basket and off the ship. If this pig got her legs poked through the basket, there was going to be utter chaos. My full attention was on the sling load of rice we were carrying. The pig managed to poke her legs and head through the basket and started running all over the helicopter. I yelled at DJ to grab the pig.

DJ looked at me in shock and said, "I don't wanna touch that pig."

"But you're an old farm boy from Texas, aren't you?"

"I worked for a crop duster. I took care of the plane."

"That's closer to a farm than I was. I was raised on the south side of Chicago. Bacon was in a package." I looked at Kenny, the left gunner, and told him to grab the pig.

"No, no, no, I won't. I don't want anything to do with that pig."

"But you're a Texas boy; you musta worked on the farm."

"I worked in a hardware store. Feed and grain mostly."

"That's close enough. Get that fucking pig."

The pig headed for the cockpit. DJ and I ran for the cockpit and grabbed the hind legs of the pig. The pilots started yelling, "Chief, Chief, there's a pig in the cockpit with us!" We pulled the pig out of the cockpit, back into the main section of the aircraft. The villagers grabbed the pig and tried to calm her down, but the pig broke free and raced to the back of the aircraft where she fell through the cargo trap door, plunging three thousand feet. DJ and I watched as the pig fell to the ground.

DJ said, "Throw two eggs down and we can have ham and scrambled eggs."

I notified the pilots that the pig had fallen out.

They said, "Just as well, he was a hazard to the operation of an aircraft." I made notes in my logbook before we took off and after we landed: the cage was substandard for the pig. The villagers had assured me the cage would hold; it hadn't. We filled out incident reports when we got back to base camp. We closed up the ship and dropped off the forms at the flight shanty and headed for the mess hall.

DJ was flustered about what had happened with the pig. He said, "In the last six months we've lost a 105 howitzer and a goddamn pig. This does not sound good for our military careers."

"You don't have a military career; you're getting out when you leave Vietnam."

"I was actually thinking of *your* military career."

"I don't have a military career. I'm getting out in a year or so."

"You should stay in and go aviation."

"Why? You just said I dropped a cannon and a pig."

"You're good at this shit, Chief. If you hadn't gotten rid of that cannon we would have been splattered all over the countryside. The pig was a pain in the ass. It was a danger to everyone. Let's go to the mess hall, I'm starving. Maybe they'll have pork for dinner."

After dinner I went back to my hooch and thought about the letter, when I was interrupted by the arrival of some friends. Of course, most of the guys had heard about the pig incident.

One of them commented, "Hey Tom, don't forget about the pig roast this Sunday. For breakfast we're having ham and eggs. And listen, I have a craving for a ham sandwich."

I couldn't resist it myself. I chimed in, "Tomorrow's movie is *Pygmalion*, or *The Pig and I*."

By the way, I was cleared of any wrong doing.

15

LESSONS LEARNED
FROM DAYS PAST

T hE NEXT DAY WE WERE HEADED NORTH PAST An Khe, but to do that we had to go through the Mang Yang Pass. This was where the last great battle of the First Indochina War had taken place. The French were pulling back, trying to get to Pleiku. In order to do that, they had to go through the Mang Yang Pass. This was also called the Battle of An Khe. The French lost about two hundred men. Legend has it they were buried on their knees facing toward France. Whenever we flew through the pass I would look for the small mounds of dirt that represented the graves of the French soldiers.

This was a grim reminder that we were up against a determined enemy. Therefore, you had to respect them and learn from them. If you didn't, you might have a mound of your own.

Highway 19 was the only land route you could take from Pleiku to An Khe. When convoys went through, there was always plenty of air cover. When the NVA or Viet Cong engaged the

Americans in combat, they would stay close to the Americans so we couldn't use our air support or artillery. So the Americans developed a strategy using helicopter gunships to support ground forces. Huey helicopters were outfitted with 20mm cannons and mini guns. Later on in the war, Bell Helicopter developed the Cobra gunship. The Cobras were also armed with 20mm cannons and mini guns. These gunships proved very effective in close-quarter combat. Vietnam is often called the "Helicopter War" and was the proving ground for helicopter technology.

****

In Vietnam, there were almost no roads. If you wanted to go somewhere, you had to hop on a chopper, which could be really scary for an infantry soldier. His thinking was, *I'm gonna fight this war with his two feet on the ground.* This was not to be. The Army in its wisdom started developing Air Cavalry units, which were nothing more than infantry in helicopters. The Army was down to one full Paratroop division, the 82nd. The 101st and 173rd were Air Cavalry Divisions. During one paratroop jump in Vietnam, the 173rd suffered a thirty percent casualty rate. After that, they decided the terrain was not favorable for jumping.

At the beginning of the war, the jungle tactics the Americans utilized proved out of date and ineffective. Once again, we had to learn from our enemies. Long Range Reconnaissance Patrols (LRRP) and Recondo schools were established.

The LRRP teams were four- or five-man teams trained to live in the jungle and dropped there by helicopters to seek out the enemy and report by radio the position and strength of the force.

They would watch the enemy for a couple of days, tracking them to their next destination. This was very hazardous duty. If they were discovered, they had to run back to a predetermined point where a helicopter would pick them up. If the enemy was too close to the LRRP team at the pick-up point they would have to go to the next selected LZ (Landing Zone). These teams were the eyes and ears of the larger divisions like the 1st Cav and the 4th Divisions.

This was not the kind of job I wanted. You had to have balls made of brass to do this kind of work. These guys would sleep under the stars every night. No tent, cold food, no washing for days. They could run all day. I admired these guys for what they did. Then again, they all thought I was nuts for riding around in a helicopter all day. All the infantry guys were so good at what they did. People back home just didn't know how good these kids were. I couldn't do what they did, but I was damn proud I knew them.

16

GETTING SHORT

THE TERM "GETTING SHORT" WAS USED WHEN your time in-
country was coming to an end. My time remaining was now
less than two months. Many G.I.s would make up humorous sayings
such as, "I'm so short I can sit on a newspaper and dangle my legs,"
or, "I'm so short I have to stand on a nickel to piss on a dime."
Everyone laughed, but in reality there was mental pressure on you.
This pressure was so heavy you would probably choose to live in a
bomb shelter for the next two months if they would let you.

This was the time you didn't hope for a milk run; you *prayed*
for one. On the outside you played the bravado thing, trying not
to look too agitated. You started doing things like checking the
aircraft two or three times. If you serviced or did maintenance on
the aircraft you checked everyone's work two or three times. You
knew exactly what you were doing and you hated yourself for
doing it. I didn't want my aircraft to fall out of the sky due to
carelessness.

You knew the people who were getting short, and if you didn't,
they would tell you. When a bunch of us were in line at the mess

hall, we would hear someone yell, "SHORT!" Why they did that I didn't know. Well, I did know; it was because they were rubbing it in. Every once in a while you would run into a guy with dark green fatigues, and you would ask him how much time he had to go. He would say, "I got 345 days to go." Then we would say, "You poor bastard, just go walk into a Huey tail rotor right now." Of course we were kidding.

We called the new guys "cherries." After about a month in-country, we finally learned their names. Some guys remained cherries. They didn't know what to do, they didn't know where to go, or how to do their job. They should have brought their mothers with them to Vietnam.

Tom Messenger, age 20, in his flight suit near barracks in Pleiku, Vietnam, 1970.

This page: (Top) Tom personalizing his aircraft *Chicago Transit; (Bottom)* With his crew chief, Byron Raney (*right*), running up aircraft for engine test. *Opposite, top*: Checking blades; *Bottom,* Tom and Byron admiring their work on *Shrimpboat 528* inside a revetment, Phubai, Vietnam, 1971.

Shrimpboat 528 with a sling load, a 105 cannon, moving towards firebase delta near Laos, March, 1971. (*Photo courtesy of Steve Richter*)

Tom was a gunner on this chinook, 6816021, with flight engineer Stan Neckermann in Pleiku, Vietnam, September, 1970. (*Photo courtesy of Stan Neckermann*)

Tom on R&R in Sydney, Australia, May, 1971.

Tom (*standing in background, left*) and his gunner, Gene Womack (*background, to the right of Tom*), persuading Cambodian refugees to board their Chinook and move to a safe camp in Vietnam from an area called the Cambodian Sanctuary, 1971. (*Photo courtesy of Eugene Womack*)

17

A DOSE OF TRUTH
AND A LITTLE TRICKERY

IT WAS TIME TO LOOK AT THE LETTER from Jack Mansky's girlfriend again, and nothing had changed. It was time to do something, because Jack wasn't getting any better. I heard Jack outside. He was done with his shit burning detail, so I asked him to come into my hooch. I told Jack to sit down and have a soda. I was wondering if I should do my best Ward Cleaver impersonation. I decided not to do that. Instead, I said, "Jack would you ever lie for me?"

"Hell no, I ain't lying for you or anyone else, unless maybe if it was life or death."

"You know I wouldn't lie for you either. You wouldn't want me to, right?"

"Right. Where's this going?"

"Last week I got a letter from your girlfriend."

"What's she doing writing to you?"

"I think you already know the answer to that."

"No, I don't! Why's she writing to you?"

"Jack, she wants to know if you're on drugs."

"What makes her suspect that?"

"Your last couple letters have been a little goofy. Read the letter yourself." Jack did, and gave it back to me.

He looked at me and said, "You could lie for me."

"I could, but that wouldn't help you. I think you should go on the amnesty program."

"What are my options?"

"You have to admit you're a drug addict; you have to enter a thirty-day detox program. Afterwards, you go home and get an honorable discharge."

"Will I get to go back on flight status?"

"I don't think so."

"What's the upside?"

"You get clean, you get an honorable discharge, you get to go home, you get to see your girl. And oh yes, you get to take a regular bowel movement like normal people."

"I used to have my own Chinook."

"I know, I know. Go on the amnesty program and see where it leads."

"I had a Chinook, I was a flight engineer, I was on flight status. Maybe the Army will make a deal."

"I don't think so; this is the deal."

"You have a Chinook."

"I do have a Chinook, but I don't have a girlfriend. Don't lose your girlfriend over this."

"So you're gonna write my girl and tell her I'm going to rehab?"

"No, you are."

"Well, if I'm not gonna tell her, and if you're not gonna tell her, then she's gonna figure it out."

"Probably."

"How come you don't have a girlfriend?"

"Long story. We broke up before I enlisted. It worked out for the best."

"Looks like I got some thinking to do. How do I get started?"

"Just go to the orderly room and fill out an application. Just do it, ya fuck head."

"If I go to detox will you come see me?"

"If they let me, yes, I will. Now get out of here so I can get to sleep. I have to fly tomorrow."

"Wish I could fly with you."

"So do I, Jack, but you have shit to burn tomorrow and an application to fill out."

Jack left and I had time to think. *How do you make somebody do something they don't want to do? How do you make someone go to rehab?* I actually got tired of thinking about it and drifted off to sleep. I was awakened at five in the morning by the CQ. I got dressed, shaved and brushed my teeth.

I walked over to the mess hall and stood in line with the rest of the flight crews. The Mess Hall Sergeant came over to me and said, "Tom, we have bacon today to go with your eggs. I don't know where the bacon came from, it's like it fell out of the sky. Oh my gosh, it did fall out of the sky!" Everyone had a good laugh. Even I did. I looked over at the officers section and saw the Old Man having a good chuckle at my expense.

I walked over to the Old Man and said, "Sir, are you enjoying your breakfast?"

"Why yes, I am, Specialist; thank you for asking. I hear we have you to thank for the bacon."

"Well, sir, enjoy your bacon, sir."

"Specialist, have a good mission."

"Thank you, sir."

I picked up my flight gear, left the mess hall, and headed for the flight line. I was met outside the door by Captain Myerson, the reenlistment officer. He said, "Good morning, Messenger. I've been looking for you. I need fifteen minutes of your time."

"Sir, I really don't have the time right now. I have a mission to get ready for."

"We have to talk about your reenlistment and the terms of the contract."

"We have nothing to talk about because there isn't going to be any reenlistment."

"You haven't heard the terms. Just give me ten minutes of your time." We went back into the mess hall and sat down at a table.

I said, "OK, shoot; let's hear what you've got to say."

"Here's the deal. You re-up for six years; the government gives you ten thousand dollars and promotes you to specialist six or staff sergeant."

"What's the catch?"

"The catch is, when your duty is done here, you go home for thirty days and then you come back to Vietnam for another tour of duty."

"No way in hell that's gonna happen." I got up and walked out of the mess hall and onto the flight line with Myerson tagging behind me.

"Well, what are you looking for?"

"How about I go home after my tour and then I go to flight school after that, and then I go back to Vietnam."

"You do know the ten thousand dollars is tax-free in Vietnam."

"What about the flight school?"

"I'll work on that."

"You do that. Let me know what you find out."

To be honest, I didn't want to re-up, but if the Army threw flight school in with the deal the offer would be very tempting and hard to refuse. I now had something else to think about. Can you imagine going home for thirty days, then coming back to Vietnam to do another one-year tour? In all honesty, I didn't want to press my luck. The way I was thinking, I had come to Vietnam with nine lives and I might leave with three. I had all this crap to think about and I had to try to walk around looking normal.

18

THE EXTRACTION

I GOT TO MY AIRCRAFT AND OPENED IT UP FOR preflight inspection. The technical inspector came up to me and told me one of the oil samples I had taken last week on the aft transmission showed signs of metal shavings. Every twenty-five hours of flight time we took oil samples from engines and transmissions and changed oil and cleaned filters.

I took another oil sample from the aft transmission and gave it to him. He marked a red "X" in the logbook and said, "Don't go anywhere till you hear from me." When he red X'd the aircraft, that meant we were grounded and waiting on the findings of the new oil samples.

All we could do was wait for the inspector to OK us for flight, or we might have to replace the aft transmission, which was an all-day-and-some-of-the-night job. The pilots left for the flight shanty (Operations), and the crew stayed with the ship. DJ and Kenny decided to catch up on their sleep.

I was trying to finish a Mickey Spillane mystery. His main character was a guy named Mike Hammer; a big, ugly private dick that got all the girls. Like that could happen. Every girl he met he called "doll." Their legs went on forever, their necklines plunged to the floor, their perfume kept a thirty-foot perimeter around them wherever they walked. If you weren't seduced by their looks, you were by the enchanting aroma. This guy Spillane could write.

The mental imagery I projected in my mind made me homesick for the United States...or Australia. I laid the book down across my chest and tried to think about my last R&R "down under." I fell fast asleep. Most crewmembers don't sleep well. You catch sleep whenever you can. Four hours during the night and maybe two hours during the day. It has something to do with being constantly alert and constantly vigilant.

I was awakened by the technical inspector walking up the ramp of the Chinook. He cleared us for flight and signed off on the red X in the logbook. When the pilots came on board we hurried up, started our engines, went through the checklist, and performed a test flight. We were OK for takeoff around 4:30. We picked up sorties of C-rations and water and took them out to the field near Kontum. We did three more of these missions. When we finished, we were cleared to go back to Camp Holloway. I thought we were to have an easy day.

Pilots have a habit of being bearers of bad news. If you're not monitoring the radios on your headset, you're listening to Armed Forces Radio, which is usually rock and roll music. For some reason, I was listening in to what the pilots were talking about. They made it very clear that we had been diverted to do an emergency extraction.

Extraction is a timing mission to pick up a small band of troops in the jungle. Usually Hueys did this kind of mission. They could hold only twelve passengers, but we could haul thirty-three American soldiers. We could haul fifty Vietnamese because they weighed much less than American troops.

The way this operation worked, we would fly up and down the Laos-Vietnam border waiting for a radio contact from the Recondo patrol. They would give us one of three preselected landing zones. We would go to that site and wait for the patrol. We started flying north about four miles and turned around and headed south, and back north again. This time we were all monitoring the radios, trying to listen for a signal. The three landing zones were coded as Bravo, Indigo, and Lima. I could hear "Bravo, Bravo, Bravo" real faintly.

The pilots looked at the map and we headed for that landing zone. We didn't circle, we just landed at the zone, which was about the size of a football field. The two gunners were sent out to form a perimeter at left front and right front about thirty yards from the ship. I was sent to the six o'clock position about twenty-five yards out. We didn't shut the engines down. Everything stayed running.

A Chinook made a lot of noise when it was running full bore. It's a wonder we didn't attract a lot of attention. During the Vietnam War, the word stealth wasn't even an afterthought in Army aviation. I decided to kneel in the grass, figuring I'd be less of a target. The sun was going down, so my visibility was hampered. I took out a set of binoculars and scanned the jungle for any movement. I didn't want to think about how short I was. We were only supposed to be there five minutes and our time was up. The pilot said we'd give them another five minutes. I went back to my resting place and waited. My hands were sweating and my mouth was dry.

If I could have turned my head 360 degrees, I would have. Of all the jams I'd been in, this one seemed to be the worst. That's because it was the latest one. I started thinking about what the reenlistment officer was offering me. *Oh yeah, any more missions like this and I could make up my mind now.*

Just then, I saw some movement coming out of the jungle to the south. I notified the pilots that we had spotted them. I looked through my binoculars again and noticed they were running at full speed. I came out to meet them and I asked this shave tail butter bar lieutenant, "Sir, why are you running?"

He said, "Chief, they are right behind us."

I said, "Oh, you brought guests." Then it was my turn to run. I motioned the gunners to get into the aircraft. The pilots asked me how close the enemy was. I said, "Close enough to be passengers." We all boarded at a dead run. I counted heads real quick and put the ramp up. I told the pilots we could leave now. The pilots pulled pitch and we were out of there in a flash. The gunners threw grenades to leave a calling card.

We dropped the patrol off at Pleiku. The butter bar was the last to leave the ship. He pulled me aside and asked, "Wasn't that exciting?"

I said, "Sir, I'm getting short, so everything is exciting. I take a crap, it's exciting. I eat a meal in the mess hall, it's exciting. I find your ass in the jungle, it's exciting. Sir."

The butter bar smiled as he walked away, stopping to say, "Next time we go hunting, I'll ask for your ship."

I didn't say anything, but under my breath I muttered, "Fucking ninety-day wonder." A ninety-day wonder was a college graduate who went into the Army and signed up for OCS (Officer Candidate School). After ninety days he graduated as a second lieutenant. That was a scary situation.

When a butter bar was put in charge, he told you what to do, and then you looked to the NCO to find out what *really* to do. It wasn't an insult, but you wanted to go with experience in that particular situation. An inexperienced lieutenant might ask the men to take a heavily fortified hill. The soldiers would look to the NCO for advice. The NCO would respectfully recommend close air support, or some artillery on the hill. The more experienced person usually made more sense in the field of battle. The lieutenant would catch on very quickly. People were constantly training and learning in the Army.

19

WHY WE DID
WHAT WE DID

WHY DID AN INFANTRY MAN WALK INTO A JUNGLE and walk out seven days later? Why did a guy drive a tank into battle, taking all kinds of fire and dishing out plenty of fire himself? Why did pilots fly over Hanoi through murderous anti-aircraft fire to drop their bombs?

Helicopter pilots and flight crews were flying in and out of danger every day. Artillery men lived on top of mountains for months in bunkers to protect other firebases. The answer was simple: For God and country. That would be their answer ninety percent of the time. We were doing this because our country asked us to. The other ten percent liked doing what they were doing and wanted to continue doing it. Sometimes I ran into people who were on their second and third tours and I'd ask why. The response was always the same: "Because I like it. I like walking in the jungle searching for NVA. I like flying jets at Mach 1. I like driving a tank and blowing things up. I like crewing on a helicopter, flying all over the country…."

Every once in a while, a guy named Tony Fowler would stop by my hooch to talk and drink some of my bourbon. Tony was on his third tour in Vietnam. He was married to a Vietnamese girl. Every time he left Vietnam she would leave also. They had lived in the States for a year, and when he had been sent back to Vietnam, she had come back and lived off post. I thought this was very strange. His wife's name was Kim. She got a job on post as a hooch maid.

So I asked Tony, "Why are you back for a third tour?" He said he was a flight engineer on the fastest, most powerful helicopter in the world. It was a five million dollar aircraft he got to take care of and fly with wherever it went. For a poor boy like him, this was as good as it was ever gonna get. He liked doing what he was doing.

He asked me, "How about you, Tom?"

I replied, "I do like it, but not enough to re-up and keep coming back to Vietnam."

"So you're getting out."

"I am, but I'm gonna think long and hard about it."

So Tony was here because he had a wife and he loved his job. I guess all this worked for them. What would happen when the war came to an end? I asked Tony, and he said they would deal with that when it came along. There's always another war, and he was right. America, how it loves its wars. They're almost a national pastime.

The only thing Tony had to watch for was the Viet Cong finding out that Kim was married to an American soldier. He would often sneak off the post on the weekends to see his wife. This was very dangerous, because like I said before, the Viet Cong had control of the town at night.

One time, Kim was scheduled to go see her family in Qui Nhon, and also to see her personal doctor because she had not been feeling well. She told Tony she would be gone for two days. When Kim had been gone for three days and he hadn't heard a word from her, he got worried. Tony was talking about taking a jeep and driving the road to Qui Nhon to see if he could find her. He was talking to three of us flight engineers.

We came up with an idea: since we were all flying out the next day, we would ask the pilots to fly over the road going to Qui Nhon. We also had friends in the 189th Ghost Riders next door to us. We knew it was going to cost us. We moseyed over to the 189th flight line and asked them to take a run to Qui Nhon, and to follow the road real close to look for any foul play.

Two warrant officers wanted to know what was going on. The one pilot was a real dickhead named Blankenfelder. He was a hell of a pilot and he thought the aircraft belonged to him.

He looked at us and said, "Well, you boys are in a pickle; this might cost you." All three of us stared that motherfucker down. He finally relented and agreed to go looking. We breathed a sigh of relief. Besides, we were all out of bribing liquid: aka, Scotch.

Civilian communication between Qui Nhon and Pleiku was horseshit, so if she was in trouble, she wouldn't have been able to get in touch with Tony. The Hueys took off for Qui Nhon and searched the main roads and found nothing. Now she was four days missing and Tony was getting frantic.

The next day we were scheduled to fly to An Khe. I was hoping to talk the pilots into a side trip to Qui Nhon. DJ looked down the flight line and asked me who these guys were coming down the flight line. I saw they were not the pilots we were supposed to have. One guy was huge. It was the Old Man, and with him was instructor pilot Dillard.

"That can't be the Old Man, he never flies with us," someone said.

"Well, it is," I said. " And we can forget about going to Qui Nhon."

Damn, if we didn't have bad luck we wouldn't have any luck at all. Talk about sticking it in our asses. Major John Haymeyer was company commander of the 179th aviation ASHC. He always went by the book but he was a fair man. They boarded the ship and greeted us on the ramp.

The Old Man said, "Good morning, Chief."

I said, "Good morning, sir. Where would you like to go today?"

"We are going to Qui Nhon. I have some business to attend to with S2 (Intelligence). While I'm gone, you gentleman can grab lunch."

I smiled to myself and thought it almost seemed like he knew what was going on. The Major turned to me and said, "Chief, why are you smiling?"

"No reason, just glad to have you on board, sir."

We flew over the main road leading to Qui Nhon and saw nothing. We landed at Qui Nhon.

The Major left the aircraft and stopped at the ramp and said, "Gentlemen, you are confined to the base till I get back." Well, that pretty much did us in. I was sure he knew my plan. We took a jeep to the mess hall and had a nice lunch. We got back to the ship and decided to sweep out the ship and make it presentable for the Old Man. The Major drove up in a jeep with Dillard. I stood up and acknowledged his presence. In Vietnam, you did not salute an officer for fear of identifying them to the enemy who liked to pick off officers before enlisted men. The Major told us to sit down and proceeded to tell us about his visit to Qui Nhon. He had gone to S2 and asked about Kim. Of course, we acted like *What the fuck was he talking about?*

He then said, "Intelligence found Tony's wife in a civilian hospital recovering from appendicitis. She will be back in Pleiku in a couple of days." The Major walked over to me and said, "Messenger, rank does have its privileges. "

I smiled and replied, "It sure does, sir; it sure does."

We flew back to Pleiku, feeling pretty good for ourselves and for Tony and his wife. The pilots and I did the post-flight inspection and closed up the ship for the night. Once again, DJ and I were the last to leave the ship. DJ and I started walking down the flight line and DJ started pissing and moaning.

"That old coot out-connived and outmaneuvered us," he said.

I said, "He just flat-out kicked our asses."

"He's a major, he's been playing this game a long time."

"What bothers me is all the colonels and generals, those bastards really know how to connive and outmaneuver us. Makes you think. I'm glad they're on our side."

DJ said, "Yeah, what was all that shit he was whispering in your ear?"

"He was just saying anything I came up with, he could do better."

"That old coot; I hate him."

"No, you don't, DJ."

"Yeah, you're right. That old coot is pretty cool. See, I love flying Chinooks. You get to do cool stuff."

"Maybe you should re-up," I suggested.

"Fuck you. I'm done."

Flying Chinooks *was* cool, and that just showed that we weren't only doing this for God and country.

Tony met us at the end of the flight line and thanked us for finding his wife. We told him we didn't find her; the Old Man did.

"Well I just saw him, and he said I have some really good friends."

DJ said, "No way, that old coot out-connived us and got intelligence to find her."

It's true that the Old Man taught us a lesson, but he also solved a problem for one of his men and that was a good thing. I, for one, admired him for this selfless act. I went back to the hooch and tried to find a bottle of bourbon to pay off the helicopter pilots who had gone searching for Tony's wife. I found a half bottle and decided to drink it myself. I looked up and there, standing in the doorway, were the two pilots. I poured three drinks and then six and then nine. It was gone, but that was OK because they had earned it.

20

THE AMNESTY OF
JACK MANSKY

I WAS STILL FLYING DAILY MISSIONS, HOPING THE DAYS would go faster. It was better to fly missions every day than to sit around waiting with nothing to do, but you did risk getting your ass shot off. I was willing to take that chance.

We returned from supporting the 25th Infantry near Doc To. We landed back at Camp Holloway, shut down the engines, performed a post-flight inspection, and closed up the aircraft for the night. I was walking down the flight line and in the middle of the taxiway was Jack Mansky, doubled over in pain with cramps. He was shaking all over and asked me to take him into the amnesty program.

I replied, "Jack, this is no bullshit. You gotta go do this right now." I had no experience in this type of thing, so I thought I had better take him *right fucking now*. I hopped into the flight platoon jeep and headed for the Dispensary to get him signed up. After that, I took him to where he would spend the next month in detox.

That was as far as I could go. Jack had tears in his eyes. He told me he was sorry he had let me down.

I said, "Jack, just get well again and come back." By then we both had tears running down our faces. Two combat veterans bawling like babies. I asked the nurse when I could visit him, and was told in three weeks.

He said, "Come visit me and bring me some smokes. And don't write my girlfriend. I want to be clean and sober when I see her." We hugged each other and they took him away.

I had four more weeks of flying left, and two weeks to clear the post. I thought about going into downtown Pleiku for one more blast, to say goodbye to the massage therapists, the Madam K's, the bartenders. Maybe, just maybe, get one more crack at the cowboys. I thought about it for a while and decided against it. I was so close to going home, why press my luck? I got back to the hooch and decided to get into a Milo March detective novel. Probably another private dick who got all the trim he could handle. I was asleep with the book covering my face when DJ came into my hooch, talking about that kid, Coley Van Kamppen.

I said, "What about that kid?"

"He keeps borrowing money to go into town to get his pipes cleaned out."

"Everyone does that."

"Not every day. He fell in love with one of those whores."

"He goes every day? No wonder he's borrowing money."

"That's not the bad part."

"What's the bad part?"

"He's staying overnight way too much."

"Why are you telling me this?"

"Because he's coming to borrow money from you, and here he is."

"Hi Coley, what's up?" I said,

"Hey Chief, I need to borrow some money. I need to go see my girl in town tomorrow."

"Are you still seeing that girl at the steam and cream?"

"Yep. We're still dating."

"You do realize you're dating a prostitute, don't you?"

"She told me she quit doing that."

"You do realize, you're dating a lying prostitute. She's probably been with two hundred men, and that's a low figure."

"She told me twenty guys."

"No, that figure is way too low. Look, kid, you're away from home for the first time and your mother and father can't see what you're doing. You're just not thinking straight right now. It's okay to be with a prostitute, blow your load, and move on. You're not supposed to fall in love with them. Is anything I'm saying getting through?"

"All I know is I want to be with her."

"That's because you're thinking with your little head instead of your big head. This is not the type of woman you take home to mother."

"You sound just like my father."

"Really? I was trying not to."

Coley turned on his heels and stomped out of my hooch like a teenager who was denied the keys to his father's car. In one small flash of time, I saw myself as Coley. That was me one year ago. Now it was me denying him the keys to the car. He wasn't going to go to Pleiku to have his pleasure. This was a defining moment for me, also. Men don't know the exact moment they become a man and reach maturity. I think it's a gradual process that takes some men longer than others.

****

Things were finally looking good. Jack was in rehab, I wasn't getting letters from his girlfriend, and I had four weeks of flying left to go. All my worries and phobias were still with me, however. I would inspect the aircraft two or three times. If I replaced a part or serviced the aircraft, I checked it out over and over again. DJ must have thought I was nuts or paranoid. If you fly every day, the days go by fast. If you fly as a standby crew, the days crawl by.

With two weeks to go, I was feeling really good about myself. I was getting the feeling I was going to make it home. Remember what I said about flying on Chinooks because I loved it so? I was just bullshitting myself. I did love flying, but the real reason was, you did it for God and country. Let me repeat: You did it for God and country.

21

THAT DAY

W E HAD JUST FINISHED A COUPLE OF MILK RUNS and landed back at Pleiku when we were summoned to the company commander's office. I looked to DJ and said, "What did you do now?

He replied, "I didn't do anything."

I said, "Maybe it's about reenlisting or extending in-country. They don't need two of us for that, because I'm going home in six weeks."

"Maybe somebody in town complained."

"Like who?"

"Maybe some of those whores you were screwing around with."

"I don't think so. I'm guessing some of the cowboys are complaining about their motorcycles getting damaged."

We cooled our heels for about ten minutes. Then the executive officer (XO) led us to the Old Man. He ordered us to come to attention, which is unusual in a combat theater. We smartly came to attention. I thought to myself, *What the hell is going on?*

The XO started reading from a sheet of paper: "For heroism while in flight on or about March 17, 1971, while participating in the Lamson 719 campaign in the Kingdom of Laos..."

He then continued on his own, "You two crewmembers of *Shrimpboat 528* have been awarded the Distinguished Flying Cross."

He went on and on about what had happened that day. DJ and I were stunned. We could barely speak. The Old Man came over to us, shook our hands, and said how proud he was of us.

I struggled to get out the words, "Thank you, sir, thank you." He told us we would get our medals at our next duty station in the States. We left the orderly room and didn't speak until we got to the flight line.

I said to DJ, "I remember that day vividly, and I can tell you right now, everything went wrong that could go wrong."

DJ said, "Maybe they have us mixed up with somebody else."

"Yeah, you're right. Let's just keep this between ourselves and not tell anyone. That way when they correct the problem we won't look like a bunch of knuckle heads."

I know this sounds crazy, but I remember that day very well. We took mortar rounds, rockets, and small arms that day. We loaded wounded under fire, and to top it off, we lost an engine and kept flying. Things were really bad that day and DJ and I were there to make it right. That day we performed our duties better than anybody in the world could do. That day two people were in the right place at the right time. That day we had two of the best pilots we could ever have. We were kind of amazed we were getting these medals. We were so busy doing our jobs and trying to fulfill our mission that we didn't take notice what it would look like from someone else's viewpoint. It was so hard to explain to people what had happened.

So DJ and I kept quiet about the mission and went about our

business like nothing had ever happened. We thought we were going to get away with it. That day would always remain in my mind.

Years later, DJ called me on the phone and said, "Remember that day in Laos? They tried to kill us that day, but they couldn't."

"Nothing could kill us that day," I said. Forty-three years later, we talked about that day. Tears rolled down our cheeks and our voices quivered talking about that day. Deep down inside, we are thankful for what we have: great wives and kids. I think DJ and I were just glad to make it out alive. Did it change our lives at all? Did it make us want to stop and smell the roses or give us a new outlook on life? I usually answer: "You mean, besides the nightmares, night sweats, and flashbacks?" Not really. Bad things happened that day and two ordinary people did something extraordinarily well.

22

THE LAST MISSION

NOW DJ AND I THOUGHT WE WERE GOING TO BE able to keep the medal story quiet, but UPI service picked up on the story and the small, local papers in Chicago and Houston ran the story. Our parents were writing letters every day, demanding to know what was going on. They were all excited. I was getting letters from people I had never received letters from before. I took all the letters and threw them in the place I threw things whenever I didn't want to deal with them—the back of my locker.

The day before the last mission, I went to see Jack, like I had promised. The guards led me into a large living room decorated with large pillows on the floor and weird, psychedelic posters on the wall. Jack came into the room with a large grin on his face, happy to see me. The drug was totally out of his system and he looked terrific, like some demon had left his body and he was at peace with himself. I was amazed at the transformation.

He was the one who spoke first. "Hey, Tommy, you look tired, man."

I replied, "I'm still working. You get to lay around and go to counseling and read books. Some of us are still fighting a war."

"I know. It's pretty boring here. I feel so much better now. I'm eating better and exercising, which leads to daily bowel movements."

Jack started talking about everything he could think of. He was starved for conversation. He kept talking about his childhood and how great it was and his family and how great they were. He was writing his girlfriend every day, not mentioning his predicament. After babbling on about everyone and everything he stopped in the middle of a sentence and said, "Are you done flying?"

I said, "No, tomorrow is my last mission."

"Are you scared?"

"Yes I am, Jack. But let's talk about you."

"You're right. It looks like my girlfriend and I are gonna get married when I get back." And I'm thinking *Jack needs to get clean.* But he interrupts my thought and says, "Maybe they'll give you a milk run."

I said, "Could be, Jack, could be."

"I wish I was going with you just one last mission."

"That's not gonna happen, Jack. You got a second chance; don't screw it up now."

All the talking was done. We both got up and hugged each other with tears rolling down our cheeks and said our goodbyes. I opened the door to leave and I could hear Jack say, "I just wanna fly left gun one more time. Just one more time."

I turned and walked away, thinking I would never see Jack Mansky again. I was right. I would never try to contact him and he never tried to contact me. That's the way the Army is. You meet people and then they leave or you leave. It happened over and over again. In my mind, Jack went back to the States clean and sober, got married, had a family and lived a great life. If I started looking for the truth maybe I wouldn't like what I found.

I got back to the company area and waiting for me in my hooch was the re-up NCO.

He said, "Well, Messenger, tomorrow is your last mission."

I said, "My last mission in Vietnam."

"Why don't you go home for thirty days and then come back to Vietnam and do another year? Then you will be out of the Army after one year instead of doing fifteen months Stateside."

"No thanks. I'm going home."

"This is where the action is for an adrenalin junky like you. You won't get missions like here in the States. If you go back to the States, your flying days will be over. You will die of boredom on some maintenance team fixing Chinooks instead of crewing on them. You will be standing inspections, cleaning helicopters until you can't stand it any longer."

"No thanks. I think I'm ready for a little boredom."

"You go home for thirty days, come back here for one year and I'll arrange it so you'll get two R&Rs. One out of country and one in-country. I'll send you to the 180th, because the 179th is standing down in four weeks."

"Sarge, I'm going home for good."

"Kid, I'm telling you you're making a big mistake."

I told him I was going home and never coming back. With that, he turned and left my hooch, shaking his head in bewilderment. I actually liked the guy. He was a grizzled old veteran just doing his job, marking time until he retired. He had fought in two wars: Korea and Vietnam.

I had a nightcap before I turned in. Everybody knew it was my last mission tomorrow and nobody wanted to talk about it. This was fine with me, because I didn't want to talk about it either. I slept well and didn't wake up until the CQ woke me up with a quick jerk of the covers.

He whispered, "Get up, you're flying." I swung my feet onto the floor, got dressed, went to the latrine, shaved and brushed my teeth, and headed into the mess hall. I ate eggs and bacon and hash browns and drank two cups of coffee. No one spoke to me as I ate my breakfast.

How odd, I thought, maybe they don't want to jinx me. Flight crews are a superstitious bunch. DJ pulled up a chair and looked at me and said, "Well, this is it. Two weeks from tomorrow you'll be on that freedom bird heading back to the world." It was impossible not to think about that freedom bird. I knew I had to really focus on the next mission.

We headed for the flight line together for the last time. We picked up the left gunner at the ship, which happened to be the kid from Canada, Coley Van Kamppen. I was surprisingly quiet and relaxed. I didn't have to tell anybody to do their job. DJ and I opened the ship for preflight inspection, checking for any discrepancies or anything that was out of the ordinary. The pilots went through their inspection and found nothing. We closed up all the inspection panels and got ready for flight.

Coley finally broke his silence and said, "I suppose you heard my girl broke up with me."

I couldn't help myself any longer. I blurted out, "But she was a prostitute! Nobody dates a prostitute longer than fifteen minutes. They get what they want and then they leave."

DJ came over and joined in the conversation and said, "Nobody moons over a prostitute. Does she still do that thing with her finger?"

"She does that for me and only me."

"You got a lot to learn. By the time you leave Vietnam you'll figure it all out. In the meantime, get extra ammo and clean the windshields." I wasn't in a teaching mood. I guess I was in a selfish survival mood. I knew if I could get through this last day of flying I would be grounded for two weeks and then I would be sent home.

The pilots got into the cockpit and started going through the checklist like I had heard a hundred times before. This time I was listening very hard. Everyone took their positions. The gunner positioned himself near the left front window. DJ, the crew chief, stood next to me at the #1 engine with the fire extinguisher. I put on my helmet and gloves and closed up my shirt and plugged into the communications cord. The pilot was talking to me now.

He said, "Hey Chief, ready on #1?"

I replied, "Ready, ready on #1." The large Lycoming engine started turning and finally ignited, and the twenty-seven foot blades were turning, and the body of the aircraft near the rear looked like it was doing a hula dance.

I walked over to the #2 engine and the pilot said, "Ready on #2?"

Once again I responded with, "Ready on #2 engine." Number two engine responded and it ignited and we were at normal rotor speed. I threw the chocks into the back of the aircraft and gave the pilot the all clear and we started taxing toward the runway.

I looked out my window and noticed a couple of flight crews giving me the bird. I couldn't help but smile and gave the bird right back to them. The tower gave us permission to take off and we paused for about thirty seconds and started rolling down the runway. Everyone knew I liked this kind of take off. As we reached the end of the runway, the pilots pulled thrust and we slowly rose into the sky.

The pilot said to me, "I know this is your last mission, so I thought you might like the takeoff."

I told him, "I appreciated it very much."

We were going along the Laotian border to resupply firebases with ammo and food. It seemed like I had done a hundred of these missions and I was well versed in what to do, but today was a different day. It was like I was saying goodbye to this country. I was actually saying goodbye to this kind of mission. Once I hit the States, it would be the end of taking fire from small arms weapons, rockets, and mortars. No more fast approaches and no more fast takeoffs. Flying would be by the book and FAA regulations. The Re-up Sergeant was right. I was an adrenaline junky. I was going to die from boredom.

We resupplied three firebases along the border and we headed home. It was an uneventful day. I sat near the ramp, looking at the mountains and valleys. I lit a Marlboro and peered out the window, thinking to myself, *What a beautiful country. Somehow the Americans, the French, the Chinese, the Russians, and the Japanese hadn't screwed up this part of it.*

As it turned out, this was a milquetoast mission. The real battle had taken place in my head before the last mission. I'd had a lot on my mind the last couple weeks. Much more than a typical twenty-one-year-old could handle.

We landed back at base camp and proceeded with the post flight, performed some light maintenance duties, and did all the paperwork and logs for the new flight engineer—whoever that might be. Before the crew and the pilots left, they wished me luck, and told me it had been great flying with me.

I was all alone now; just me and the lady I had courted for a year. I had taken care of her for most of that time, repairing her when she broke down, servicing her when she needed new oil and clean filters. In all reality she had never let me down; when the pilots needed extra power it was there, and plenty of it. When we were coming into a hot LZ, she held her own and could take a beating time after time. I sometimes wondered: *When she was built at the Boeing Vertol plant in Pennsylvania, did a worker somehow say a prayer as she was built and rolled off the assembly line?* Sounds silly, doesn't it? Like you had the spirit of all who had built her riding with you. I never questioned this feeling; I just went with it because it felt good.

I finished the paperwork and closed up the ship and headed for the flight shanty. As I passed the rear of my ship I patted her on the fanny near the rear ramp area and said, "Thanks for the ride ol' girl, it's been a blast." I dropped off the forms and headed to the hooch. It would be my last walk down that long flight line. It was a long walk back to the hooch. Time for one cigarette and a can of Shasta soda.

I had time to think about what had just happened and what was going to happen. I got all the action I could take for one year. The Army had lived up to its part of the bargain and I had lived up to mine. I could go home for thirty days and come back for another year, but I really wanted to go home and follow a different path. I was ready for a new journey. That's what I really liked: journeys with different destinations. I was ready. I was tired and worn out by the daily missions into dangerous and battle-scarred places in Vietnam.

23

DI DI MAU
(GETTING OUT OF HERE)

I ONLY HAD TWO WEEKS LEFT IN-COUNTRY. All I had to do was clear the Personnel Department, Finance Department, Dispensary, Judge Advocate General Office, the Orderly Room, and the Quartermaster. This usually took two weeks. In the meantime, they gave me a small, do-nothing job so I wouldn't kill or injure myself. I was actually more afraid of running into a door or playing basketball and getting whacked in the nose. I could picture it now. If I were bleeding badly, I'd have to stay a couple extra days. I didn't do any serious drinking and I certainly left the ladies of the night alone.

For the next two weeks I was the CQ. I was the NCO in charge of the company from eight o'clock at night to six o'clock the next morning. I was assigned a CQ runner, who was to wake up the flight crews in the morning at five o'clock for their missions. This was a boring job. I almost wanted to go back on flight status for the next two weeks. But this was a safe job, if I could withstand the boredom.

I had to sell my small refrigerator, my Akai M10 reel-to-reel tape player/recorder, music tapes, and a reading lamp my parents had sent me from home. I sold everything for two hundred dollars. I was back to drinking soda pop and iced tea, if I could get it. I was afraid to drink and do something foolish like break a leg or end up in the hospital with some kind of disease. As the days crept by, I kept myself busy reading more cheap detective novels and playing horseshoes. I stayed off the basketball court, thinking I would play it safe. The paranoia was setting in and there was nothing I could do about it. You can be sure there were some guys who wanted to sleep in a bunker in case of a mortar or rocket attack.

The night before I left, a few guys stopped by my hooch. We had a few drinks, told war stories, and said our goodbyes. I did not sleep well that night. I was anxious and jumpy the whole night. I finally fell asleep around three o'clock and was woken by the CQ runner at six thirty. I got dressed and headed for the mess hall and ate a breakfast of SOS (shit on a shingle), eggs, and bacon. Several more guys sat with me and wished me good luck and goodbye.

DJ came by and sat down. It was our last breakfast together. I could not have asked for a better crew chief than DJ. He was always right there when I needed him. We went nine months crewing together with never a cross word between us. When there was work to do, he was right there with me. This morning I thanked him for his loyalty to me and the ship and for all the good times and good laughs we had. I was getting a lump in my throat; it was like saying goodbye to a brother.

The Old Man came by the table and said goodbye and good luck. For some reason, I stood up and greeted him and wished him well. I also told him it was an honor serving under him.

He said, "I understand you're not coming back."

I replied, "That's right, sir. I'm not coming back." He understood and wished me well.

I finished breakfast and stood my last formation in Vietnam. Formations are for the officers to do head counts and to convey any information to you. At the end of the formation they said goodbye to whoever was leaving. You could hear guys mumbling to themselves, "Lucky motherfucker," and so on...and so on. I smiled to all of them and told them their day was coming. Then I added, "Maybe."

I walked back to my hooch and picked up my duffle bag, a small flight bag, and said goodbye to the hooch maids. My hooch maid, Lannie, walked over to me and said, "You go home now."

I repeated, "I go home now." Lannie had always taken care of me and had never stolen from me. When I came back from missions, my room was always clean, my clothes were washed and hung up, and my boots were always shined. I would give her Coca Cola or Tide detergent to take home for her family. I reached into my pocket, gave her a ten spot, and told her to take *papasan* out to dinner. She started weeping.

She leaned against me and said, "You always number one. I not want you to go."

I walked out to the company street and caught a jeep headed for the flight line. The driver pulled up in front of a small Bell Ranger helicopter. The pilot was doing a preflight and I helped him get it ready for the day's mission: taking me to Camranh Bay. After we finished the preflight, he let me fly next to him in the right seat. He started the engine. It sounded different than a Chinook. The pilots received permission to take off and we taxied to the runway. We took off down the runway, two feet off the ground, and finally gained altitude. I looked back at the flight line and saw my old ship. There was DJ, preparing it for flight. I had been the flight engineer of 18528 for the last nine months and now someone else had the job. It felt strange to see someone else at the helm.

I felt a little guilty, leaving my buddies there to fight a war as I was going home. That's the way the war in Vietnam was: men were coming in as other men were going home. Tonight, a new replacement would take my spot and the rotation kept on and on. The pilot landed near the Transition headquarters for all personnel leaving Vietnam. The pilot confided in me that he wanted to be transferred to a helicopter gunship company so he could see some action. I wished him well and good luck. Action was the last thing I wanted to see. I picked up my bags and walked over to the headquarters and checked in.

The NCO in charge looked at my papers, then told me to get in line for temporary barracks. *Another line to get into*, I thought to myself. In the Army you spend half your life in line. When I got to the front of the line, I was assigned a bed in the barracks and told where the mess hall was. The Sergeant told me to be ready to take a piss test in the morning. I had to wait around for the results of the test before I could board a jet. Maybe that would be tomorrow night. I asked what I was being tested for, but I already knew the answer. I was told I had to be clean: no heroin, cocaine, or marijuana. The NCO asked me what my drug of choice was. When I said Jim Beam, he said to get the fuck outta there.

I went to my assigned barracks, made my bed, and took a nap while waiting for the mess hall to open up. Some of the guys were real nervous. My guess was they weren't going to pass the piss test in the morning. If you couldn't pass a drug test, chances were you were going to detox that day.

I went to the mess hall, ate a hearty meal, and drank plenty of liquids. For some dumb reason, I drank two glasses of chocolate milk. There wasn't much to do so I shot baskets with a couple of guys until dark. When I crawled into bed, I fell fast asleep. I woke up at six o'clock and showered and shaved.

The MPs led us into special latrines, with armed guards watching us urinate into a small jar. Talking was not allowed. I checked the jar for my name, rank, and serial number. I urinated and put the cap back on. I put a label on it and watched it being sealed up in a cardboard box. I signed the label and the bottle and box. I was led out and back to the mess hall for breakfast.

After breakfast, there was more waiting and more waiting. I could almost tell who would pass and who wouldn't. I ran into a couple of guys I had been in aviation school with at Fort Eustis and we laid around thinking about what we would do when we got back to the world. We often referred to the United States as "the world."

We would say, "When I get back I'm going to have a juicy hamburger at Fat Johnny's on North Avenue." Or, "I want a large pizza smothered with everything and a large glass of beer." It was fun listening to guys talk about what they missed and what they were going to indulge in when they got back. These little pleasures were once taken for granted.

Of course everyone said they wanted "round eye sex" ("slant-eyed" girls were all we had seen for the past year).

And then of course there were their cars. Before a lot of the guys left home, they jacked their cars up, covered them up, and put them in storage for a year. These were their babies and they missed them.

In the late afternoon, they started calling off names and we were sent to a terminal building with all our belongings and got into another line. Our names and IDs were checked, our bags searched, and we were told to go to another line.

For some reason, I smelled jet fuel and I got real excited. I peeked out the door and noticed a United Airlines jet on the taxi way. We were ordered into another line and this time they started checking our duffel bags and luggage for any contraband or weapons. One by one, we were released to get in line for the Freedom Bird. When everyone was in line, we walked slowly out to the aircraft and were greeted by the stewardesses. Almost immediately I noticed our social graces were lacking. We were speaking in half-Vietnamese slang and half-American. We had been gone too long. We had changed in order to conform and survive in a combat theater. Now we had to change to conform to a peaceful, civilian society. I realized this as soon as I saw the stewardesses.

We got to our seats and were very anxious. Finally everyone was loaded on the large jet and the doors closed. The pilots started taxiing and got into position to take off. After the aircraft started down the runway and lifted off, we cheered loudly. We were on our way home!

After all the celebrating was over, it was time to sleep and reflect a little on what I had done for the past year. The one question that had always nagged me was, *Did I do enough and could I have done more?* It would take forty-three years to answer that question. I have never asked my fellow veteran friends if we had accomplished enough in Vietnam. Could we have done more? I never asked this question because I was afraid it might invoke an argument or hurt their feelings. I was not afraid of an argument. I felt that we had been through enough already.

I think there are two kinds of Vietnam veterans. The first kind of veteran was the angry, proud veteran who would never forget that he served and wore his heart on his sleeve. The second kind was the veteran who wanted to forget and grow his hair long and blend in with the sign of the times. It is impossible for a Vietnam veteran to forget about the war. There are just too many memories. That goes for all veterans of World War I and II, Korea, the Gulf Wars, and the war in Afghanistan. It's in our souls. It's not going anywhere. I knew we were different than the lucky G.I.s who went to Germany, Korea, or some other country during the Vietnam War. They were soldiers, but they just didn't get it because they did not serve in a combat theater.

I was tired, so I decided to sleep as long as I could because it was a twelve-hour flight to Anchorage, Alaska, and then on to Seattle and Ft. Lewis, Washington. Sleeping sitting up was not my forte, and I would sleep for about an hour and then stay awake for two hours.

Finally we landed at Anchorage and refueled. We were able to disembark, walk around, stretch our legs, and have a smoke. Most of us were anxious to get back home to see if anything had changed. You could see it on our faces and in our actions. We just weren't quite sure what lay ahead of us. I think we all would have been satisfied if nothing had changed.

The plane was refueled and it was time to get back on to finish our journey. We landed at Seattle and I took a bus to Ft. Lewis, where we waited in line for more records to be processed. I was finished processing and went to get new uniforms.

A little Chinese guy started measuring me for a new class A uniform. Because I was hard to fit, I had to wait for them to tailor-make it. In the meantime, the staff gave me a ticket to the mess hall, which was in the same building. While my new duds were being made I went to the mess hall, wearing only my underwear. On the menu, my eyes latched onto the T-Bone steak. There I was, eating a twelve-ounce steak with baked potato, garlic bread, green beans, and for dessert, strawberry shortcake. I ate my whole meal sitting in my underwear. I was surprised by how good it tasted. I had no complaints.

I went back to check on the progress of my class A uniform. After I put it on, the Chinese tailor inspected his work, and gave his approval by bowing and saying, "Very good fit." I bowed back, thanking him for doing such a great job. It was the best fitting class A uniform I ever wore in the Army.

I was released from Ft. Lewis with thirty days leave time and a whole pocket full of money. I took another bus to SeaTac airport, and took a standby flight to Chicago. I was on my way, seated in first class near a window. The stewardess was feeding me highballs the whole trip home and I was a little worse for wear. But when I landed at O'Hare airport, I was feeling good.

24

WELCOME HOME!
(SORRY, WE WENT CAMPING...)

I GOT MY LUGGAGE OFF THE CAROUSEL AND HEADED for the taxi stand with a huge grin on my face. On the lower level I ran into a bunch of protestors. They started yelling at me and calling me names: "baby killer," "murderer," and so forth. Nothing could ruin this day. I smiled and kept walking. I hailed a cab and instructed the driver to head to the south side of Chicago. I looked back at the protestors, not caring much for them. I knew later on there would be more confrontations, but tonight I didn't give a shit.

I enjoyed the ride home, down the Dan Ryan Expressway, past the Loop and all its tall buildings. On my right was Comiskey Park, home of the Chicago White Sox. I asked the driver how the Sox were doing this year.

He said, "Pretty good; they got a third base slugger named Bill Melton who's tearing up the league." It was getting dark now and I just sat back and decided to enjoy the ride. A year had gone by and I was amazed how everything had changed.

The driver pulled up in front of my house and got the bags out. There was a large banner stretched across the front yard that said, "Welcome Home Tommy!" I looked at the sign and I got a little weak-kneed. The driver shook my hand and thanked me for my service. I paid him and carried my bags into the house. I still had my house key. I was expecting a rousing "welcome home" greeting.

I shouted as loud as I could, "I'm home! Anyone here?" I turned on all the lights. Nobody was home. On the kitchen table was a large note that read: "Welcome home Tommy. We are up at the campgrounds in Michigan. The keys for the Ford are on the kitchen table." I sat down. I must admit I was a little deflated.

Just then the back door opened and my sister Suzy came in and stared at me. I think she was expecting the baby-faced brother who left a year ago. Instead, she was looking at a totally different person she couldn't describe. That's OK. She looked the same to me, except her hair was a little longer and she was wearing bell bottom blue jeans with holes in them. She told me the whole family went to Michigan on a camping trip and I was to leave as soon as possible to join them. She asked me if I was going to leave tonight and drive all night. I told her I was bushed and I needed some sleep.

I went over to the family liquor cabinet and looked for a bottle of Jim Beam. Sure enough, there it was, waiting for me to make my grand entrance. I poured myself a small drink and sipped the melted ice cubes. My sister noticed that the liquor belonged to Dad, and she told me so. I looked at her, smiled, and said, "Well, things have changed."

We stayed up till midnight talking, and when I couldn't keep my eyes open, I stumbled to my old room and lay on the bed. I looked at the White Sox pennant, the pictures of Nellie Fox, Louis Aparicio, and Jimmy Landis. They were my favorite players on the Sox team. The letterman sweater from Morgan Park High School, where I had played basketball, still hung in the closet. Pictures of all the great cars of the sixties were lining the walls of my room, just like they were before I left. There were Corvettes, Impalas, Mustangs, Chargers, the list went on and on. This was the golden era of the muscle car. My baseball bat and glove were in the usual spot in the closet. My Little League and Pony League trophies were all there. But somehow things had changed, and I didn't belong here anymore. I was too tired to figure it out. I laid my head on the pillow and dropped off to sleep.

The next morning I woke up to Mister Burger mowing his lawn. *Who does that at seven in the morning? Don't people know I just got back from Vietnam? These unpatriotic sons of bitches.* Then I looked at the clock on my nightstand. It wasn't seven o'clock; it was twelve noon! I took back what I thought about Mr. Burger.

I thought I'd go to the latrine, take a shower, shit, and shave, then hit the mess hall for breakfast. Wait a minute. There is no latrine or mess hall. This was my home and that meant that I had to make my own breakfast, because everyone was up in Michigan camping. I'd had enough of camping—eating out of cans, eating my meals in a helicopter, sleeping in a helicopter. I wanted to go to a restaurant and eat breakfast like a normal person. I took my shower, shave, and shit, and got dressed in blue jeans and a tee shirt.

Any minute now the phone was going to start ringing, with a bunch of questions: How are you? Why aren't you here? When are you coming? I hurried out of there and went to the nearest restaurant. I sat in the farthest booth with my back to wall. That way I could see everyone approaching me. The waitress came over and asked me what I wanted.

I said, "Breakfast: two eggs over easy, hash browns, bacon, crispy, and order of French toast and a cup of coffee."

She said, "OK, just one question."

I said, "What's that?"

She said, "Where'd you get that fantastic tan?"

I said, "Vietnam, the hard way."

"What's the easy way?"

"There isn't any."

It was a fantastic breakfast and I slowly ate every last bite. I drank my coffee and smoked a cigarette, relaxing as I looked out the window.

The damndest thing was, everyone was going about their business like there wasn't a war going on. This really chapped my ass. Guys were over in Southeast Asia dying and these people didn't give a shit. These people didn't deserve the great Armed Forces we had.

But I looked around the restaurant and I was definitely in a minority. The war was not affecting these people at all. I was afraid every returning vet was going to notice this and feel the same way I did. Nothing was taken away from these people for the greater good of the war.

In World War II, people had to give up or at least ration gas, rubber, cigarettes, nylons, some foods. If this war wasn't on the news at ten o'clock, they wouldn't know about it unless they had a loved one serving.

Those were some of the things I noticed first when I got back. Before I went into the service it was the same way. I looked, but I did not see. I did not notice.

I went back home and started packing a bag for Michigan. I looked around my old room and came to the conclusion that I didn't belong there anymore; as much as I wanted to, I didn't belong there. This was Tommy Messenger's room and he never came back from Vietnam. But Tom Messenger came back, and he was different. It wasn't like I couldn't sleep here anymore or stay here for a while. It was like one door closing and another door opening. Somewhere down the line, a new path was forming and I didn't know where or when it would take me.

I picked up some smokes and started my long drive to Michigan. The drive did me good, but I still wanted to get back with my friends and raise a little Cain. I pulled up into the campgrounds and there they were: a large mass of Messengers with smiles on their faces and arms stretched out. I kissed and hugged everyone in line until I was kissed and hugged out. After all the crying and laughter was over, we ate a large meal. When you and eight other siblings and two parents sit down for dinner, it looks like a banquet.

After dinner, my brothers, my dad, and I sat around the campfire roasting marshmallows and drinking beer. My oldest brother wanted to know about the Air Medal and the Distinguished Flying Cross.

I said, "Well, there's not much to tell you, it all happened so fast. All I can say is I performed very well under severe rocket and mortar fire. We were able to complete our mission under the worst battle conditions." This small synopsis satisfied my dad because he was a veteran who was at the Battle of the Bulge. He fully understood.

My oldest brother wanted more details, like something out of a Hollywood story.

"How many people did you kill?" That was the next question he asked.

Dad intervened and told my brother, "That's something you never ask a veteran." My brother changed the subject and we never talked about it ever again. Which was fine with me.

Later that night, my dad got me alone and we discussed the medals and what had happened that day in Laos. He listened very intently, not making any facial expressions or verbal comments.

He arose from his chair and spoke slowly but firmly and said, "We will not discuss this ever again. These are things you had to do. But I am proud of the way you carried yourself this last year. The medal is a symbol of the extraordinary job you did under difficult circumstances while performing your duties. I have a feeling other people are going to ask you about this. How you handle this is up to you." From that day on, my dad and I understood each other better than we ever had. The Messenger family was represented in the last four wars. We will probably answer the call in future wars.

My mother didn't want to know anything about the medal. She didn't want to know about the close calls, the dying, or the things that are done in war in the name of God and country. As far as she was concerned, I was home and nothing had changed. She was to quickly learn that I had changed and that there was nothing she could do about that. I think she thought her will as a mother was stronger than any war on earth.

My parents left for Illinois four days later. I decided to stay in Michigan and stay with my older brother. I thought that by staying with him, I could go my own way and do what I wanted to. I felt like they were watching over me, like I was going to do something drastic. I had no idea what their problem was.

I didn't have much time to think about them though, because my wisdom teeth started kicking up again, worse than ever. I started taking aspirin to kill the pain but it was no use; they had to come out. My sister-in-law Linda took me to an oral surgeon in South Bend, Indiana.

I wore my uniform and he saw the wings on my chest and asked if I was in aviation. I told him I served on CH-47 Chinooks. As it turned out, he had been a flight surgeon in World War II and had become an oral surgeon after the war.

He did a great job taking out three teeth. He wouldn't take any payment for the surgery but I insisted he take something. I was still groggy from the sodium pentothal and I needed help getting into the car. I remember I slept the better part of two days. When I woke up, I looked into my mouth and saw that my back gums were full of black thread. I did not want to spend my thirty-day leave nursing a sore mouth.

My brother kept a boat on Diamond Lake near the town of Cassopolis, Michigan, so we decided I needed some recreation and some serious girl watching. My brother and I got the boat out and got it ready for skiing. He said I should go first. I grabbed the skis and got into the water. I signaled I was ready and he pulled me out of the water. We started going around the island, but the problem was that whenever he saw a raft with women in bikinis on them sunning themselves, he would stop the boat and tell the lovely girls, "See that guy back there on the end of the rope? Well, that's my brother and he just got back from Vietnam and he is going to be awarded the Distinguished Flying Cross next month. So what do you think of that?" Then he would slowly pull me past their raft as I was dying of embarrassment.

I would say, "Hi ladies," and they would laugh and giggle. I would say, "I apologize for my brother, he has just been released from a state mental institution." More laughing and giggling. Then he would pull me up and I would start skiing again, and then he would find another raft full of woman and say the same thing. This was really the height of embarrassment for me, and I'd much rather do my own talking and embarrass myself, instead of having my brother shill for me. I understood his intentions, and he was just being a big brother. But in the last year, time had passed and I had grown more aggressive when it came to women. I knew it, but he didn't. Sometimes I think he was a little jealous because he was stuck in Niles, Michigan, and never got out before he was married and saddled with kids and responsibility. Staying on Diamond Lake seemed to revive me and put me in a good frame of mind. After four days it was time for me to go back to Illinois. I said goodbye to all my relatives in Dowagiac and Niles. I visited the VFW in Niles. It was named after La Rue Messenger. He was the first American killed in World War I. I was heading back home and I thought the long drive home would do me good. It was filled with cigarettes and rock and roll. The country had changed in the year I had been away. The people had turned against the war and the politicians and the military who ran the war. Some of the people took it out on us. All we did was what our country asked us to do.

25

OLD GIRLFRIENDS
ARE JUST THAT

I GOT HOME AND WAS GREETED BY MY PARENTS and the whole
family. This was the welcome home I had wanted. My family
was definitely on my side and they had supported me throughout
the war and after. My mother was having a hard time coming to
terms with the way I was acting. After all the celebrating had
settled down, I was usually off on my own with my friends and
sometimes I wouldn't come in till five or six the next morning.
This disturbed my mother a great deal. She was under the
impression that she was in charge and she was in control.

I woke up the next morning and she fixed me breakfast and sat
me down and said that she and my dad were very disappointed
in my behavior. They were taking away the car and they wanted
the lawn mowed and the gutters cleaned out. My mother thought
things were going to revert to the way they were before I went
into the Army. She was sadly mistaken. They had sold my 1964
Chevrolet Impala convertible because they needed the money. I

remember giving them my consent, because they were my parents. So now I needed a car, but I had to use their car because mine was sold. This was my time to kick up my heels and have a good time before I was sent back to the Army. Mom had a hard time understanding this, but Dad was a calming influence upon her. She had no idea that I had a pocket full of money and I could go buy a car. I told my mom in no uncertain terms that things were different and I was going to come and go as I pleased. This was very hard for her to take and I almost apologized right after I said it.

I said, "If you don't want me here, I'll just go to Grandma's house and stay there."

She retorted, "What makes you think she'll take you in?"

It was my turn to retort, "Why wouldn't she take in her veteran grandson?"

She had one more thing to say about the situation. She said, "I gave the United States Army a nice boy, and look what I got back." I had won a small but important victory. It was all about her letting go and realizing that I would be alright. Besides, she had six more kids to control.

****

Before I went to Vietnam I had been going out with a girl I had met in high school. Her name was Jan and she was a cute, small, athletic blonde. The first three years had been pretty hot and heavy, and it had slowly cooled down the last two years. We had made a very mature decision that we would go our own ways while I was in Vietnam. But now I was curious to find out if there was any spark left in our relationship. Her letters had been distant and noncommittal, like one friend talking to another. But still, I had to find out, person-to-person, if there was any zing left to salvage. I called her up and she sounded genuinely glad to hear from me. She wanted me to come over when it was convenient and I told her tonight would be fine and she agreed.

I hung up the phone and told my mom where I was going. She looked at me with that "I know more than you do" look that mothers have a way of conveying to their children. I looked at my sister Sue and she just rolled her eyes. Nobody could roll her eyes like my sister. They all knew more than I did. That was OK, I would know tonight if this was going any further or if I would have to go hunting again. I got duded up pretty good in civilian clothes and was met at the door by her parents. Everything seemed to be OK. I met Jan down in the basement where we could talk. The basement got icy cold, like walking into a meat locker. I tried to get a little cuddly but that didn't work. It was her turn to talk, and she told me things had changed and I wasn't in the picture anymore. It was really too bad, because she would have made a great companion. I knew a great girl was getting away, but you can't make someone like you.

I said to her, "You could have said this shit on the phone."

She said, "I know I could have, but I still wanted to see you. We have five years together, that means something."

I said, "We actually broke up when I left for Vietnam."

She said, "Vietnam actually gave us a chance to break up."

I said, "Well put. You've changed, and so have I."

I turned and started to walk away, and she blurted out, "We can still be friends." It was my turn to roll my eyes. I left out the side door like a thief in the night. This was the official end to a five-year relationship that should have ended long ago; two years ago to be exact. It had worked well in high school, but after that we had been too chicken to say goodbye. We were comfortable and convenient with each other.

I met up with some friends and we decided to go to a night club to celebrate my lightening of a load, or the termination of a relationship. I was a real free agent now. I met up with a pretty brunette I had gone to high school with. I had always had a thing for her, and she for me. I spent a lot of time with her on the dance floor. I think she was just what the doctor ordered. I took her home that night and was promised another date. I got home around three in the morning and found my mom watching late night TV and folding laundry. My dad was asleep on the couch.

Mom said, "Oh, you're home early." They knew what had happened and they wanted to know if I was alright.

I said, "Why did you stay up?"

My dad woke up and said, "Because that's what parents do. Even if you are a tough combat soldier. We were concerned."

I said, "I'm fine, and you can go to bed." So we all went to bed. I went to bed thinking about what had transpired that night. The Australians have a saying: "A Sheila broke your heart, and a Sheila can mend your heart." It was true.

****

Half of me was home and the other half was still in Vietnam. I wasn't quite sure what I was experiencing. Certain sounds bothered me. Images would flash in my head like short movies. Nightmares and night sweats were regular. I had to act differently in public. I needed to tell somebody about this. *But who, and what was this? How do I act normal? Why am I checking the door and the door locks?* I had thought that when I got home, I would sleep better. *How do I get all the way home? I'm here physically, but a lot of me is back in Vietnam. I carry this in my soul and in my mind. It's always with me and shows up at inopportune times.*

I finally fell asleep around five in the morning. I woke up around ten and lay in bed. There was no mess hall to go to and no missions to do and no helicopters to repair. I looked around my room and noticed it was a little messy; my clothes needed washing and my bed linens needed laundering. I thought to myself that the hooch maid would take care of it. Then it dawned on me: I don't have a hooch maid to clean up after me. I had paid my hooch maid six dollars a month and provided the soap to do my laundry. Who's going to do all this work for me? Not my mother; she works and takes care of the other kids. Not my sisters; they go to school and have jobs. Oh great, I don't have a maid. It looks like it's going to be me. It looks like I have to reacquaint myself with my parents' washer and dryer.

I piled everything into a basket and went downstairs and started separating the laundry into whites and darks. *This was a fine how do you do.* A combat veteran comes home from war and has to do his own laundry. In Vietnam you don't have time to do your own laundry and clean your quarters. So you hire someone to do it. The problem is, you get used to someone doing it and then you expect it. What this meant was another change I had to go through, although a small one.

****

Before I went into the Army, the regular girlfriend and I were having troubles and we were on again, off again for a whole year. This was very frustrating to me, but it had forced me to seek out other girls for relationships, because during my high school years I was a tall, lanky kid with the worst acne you ever saw. My face looked like mini volcanos, ready to erupt. I was working at Walston & Co and this is where it all started.

I met a nice Lithuanian girl from the office who took a shine to me and we started dating, so that meant I was dating two girls at the same time. This was all new to me and very exciting. Then one day I was taking the Rock Island train home and I bumped into a tall blonde and immediately was smitten with her presence and personality. We talked all the way to her stop and then the next day we rode the train together again. I found out she liked to play tennis. I told her I liked to play tennis also, which was a big fat fucking lie.

We agreed to play Wednesday night at the park. That night I went to the library and took out a book on tennis. There was one more thing I needed, and that was a tennis racket. I ran off to Sears and bought the cheapest one they had. I bought tennis balls and started practicing, hitting the ball against a wall. I was athletic enough to play this sport, I figured. I read the book and hoped I remembered the rules. We met at the park and started playing; at first I did all right, but then she started putting some fancy moves on me that I had a hard time answering. My forehand was strong, but my backhand was weak. She knew this and exploited this weakness. After years of playing baseball, my forehand was so strong I would blow it by her, but she learned to hit to my left. She beat me, but not too badly.

She walked to the net and said, "You've never played tennis before, have you?"

I said, "What gave it away?"

She said, "You were saying 'love' too much, and you couldn't counter any of my shots."

I asked, "Are you angry?"

"I should be, but I'm not."

"Why not?"

"Putting yourself through what you did to be with me was really a nice gesture and pretty cool." I was wondering why these girls were noticing me now. I had to look in the mirror to find the answer: my mini volcanos were gone. My face was cleared up and smooth again. I had tried every facial lotion known to man: Phisohex, Stridex medicated pads, Clearasil. If it was on TV, I was trying it.

I was dating three girls at the same time now and I was

euphoric and flying high from the experience. But all too soon it came crashing down. I don't know how it happened, but I came down with a sickness called mononucleosis, which is a virus that stays with you for thirty days and is spread by kissing. I was down and out for a month and all I could do was sleep. The three girls would try to visit me, but eventually they found out about each other and I was toast. The fun was over and I was back to square one, but it had been fun while it lasted. Of course, my mom had a lecture for me: "Serves you right, nobody can dangle three women at the same time."

You know, she was right. This all happened before I left for the Army. The girl from high school had let me down gently, or as gently as she could. The Lithuanian girl was always a fun girl to be with. You didn't have to prime her carburetor; she was ready to go anytime. While I was on my thirty-day leave at home, I called her house and her mom told me to come over and have dinner. I thought this was a good sign. It wasn't. I got there around five o'clock and she served me drinks, but there was no Lena.

I asked her mom, "Where is Lena?"

Her mother was very distraught, and I could not understand her because she was speaking Lithuanian. Lena's sister, Divas, had to translate. It turned out Lena had quit her job and moved to California to live and work in a commune. Later on I learned she was married to one of the guys in the commune.

The only one left now was the tennis-playing banker's daughter. I called her up and she vaguely remembered me, but she was on her way to Wellesley on the east coast. I think I had been just a plaything.

It's too bad; I liked them all, but I had been gone for a year and they had found new paths to follow, new relationships. I was not feeling too good. I lamented to my dad that everyone and everything had changed. My dad let me go on running off at the mouth, and then he decided to speak, and when he did it was slow and deliberate.

"So, you think everyone has changed and you're feeling sorry for yourself."

I replied, "Not sorry for myself, I'm just trying to fit in, that's all."

"The only person who has changed here is you. You have gone to places no one here can imagine and you have done things we could not have done. You have done a lot in one year, think about it."

My dad was right. He didn't talk much, but when he did, he chose his words well and you understood him. He had learned from his life experiences and passed them on to us. He survived World War II and was part of the Greatest Generation that saved the world. I was caught between two worlds. I could go back to Vietnam and get immediate acceptance or go on to my next duty station and gradually find friends and a social life. It didn't take me long to figure it out. I was going to my next duty station and that was final. My dad and I decided to do something we had never done before: we went to a neighborhood bar and had a beer. The second round, I asked for a Jim Beam and 7Up.

He asked, "When did you start drinking Jim Beam?"

"In Vietnam."

These wars we have. We go into them with the idea that your sons and daughters won't have to go. They end up going. Those who serve carry the war around with them. What you have to do when you come back is try to make the best life you can.

I had never seen my dad tipsy or even a little inebriated, but this afternoon was the exception. I poured him into the Ford station wagon and drove home, trying to think of an excuse for why my dad had got so drunk so fast. The only thing I could think of was he was drinking on an empty stomach.

I got him into the house and there waiting for us was my mom, with a stern look on her face. She looked at us in disgust and said, "Well you could have taken me along with you." I told her it was the men's afternoon out. My dad rose from his chair and told my mom that we would never speak of this incident again and made a motion with his hand as if to cut her off. He walked into the bathroom and turned on the water in the sink. He took his shoes and socks off and started washing his socks in the sink. I thought, *How odd.*

I turned to my mom and asked, "Why is he washing his socks in the sink?"

She said, "I don't know, but he did the same thing one other time when we lived over on 111th and May."

Right at this exact moment I realized that parents can make mistakes just like us young people growing up. It made me wonder what my parents had been like when they were young, growing up, going to parties and night clubs. They must have been fun to hang with. I always wondered why they'd had all these kids to take care of. Why do people have kids in the first place? What a burden to deal with every day. It seemed like kids just weighed you down and made life more difficult.

After Dad was finished washing his socks he went to their bedroom, crawled into bed, and fell fast asleep. I never mentioned the incident to him, although I wanted to, to give him a little dig.

I took my dad's advice and made the best of the two remaining weeks of my leave. I hooked up with the girl from the bar and had a great time with her. She was a partying girl and was always looking for a good time. So I obliged her. We ended up at an Oak Lawn motel more than once. I was just biding my time, waiting to go to my next duty station. There was no love connection, just a physical one and a lot of laughs.

Three days before I left I cut down considerably on my drinking and stayed around home and visited a few friends and relatives. I was starting to get back into shape as a soldier. I was under the impression that my flying days were over and that I would spend the rest of my hitch on a maintenance team fixing other people's Chinooks. Boy, was I was wrong. The next eighteen months were going to be a surprise, just the way I liked it.

****

More paths were opening up before me but I couldn't see them in Illinois. I would have to go to Fort Benning, Georgia, to see the next chapter in my life. The last three days at home were a time of mending fences with my mother. She did ask me one question, and that one question was, "When will I see my nice boy again?"

I told her that nice boys don't fight wars and it would be a long time until she'd see him; perhaps never. This was a hard fact of life, that war changed people and not always for the better.

She said, "I can wait." I smiled at her and started mowing the lawn, cleaning the gutters, and washing the cars. All the things she wanted done. It was a good three days.

The nights were hard because of the nightmares and night sweats. I would wake up at three in the morning and check the perimeter of the house. I was ever-vigilant, waiting for someone to enter the house. I could see in the back yard if anyone had been lurking. I could maintain my night vision like the Army had taught me. Other people were blind but I could see in the dark. It is strange, the lessons we still remember from the war. The things you hear from a distance. I can hear a mortar round leaving its tube while sound asleep. These are things you carry with you the rest of your life. You never forget them. You try, but they are ingrained in you.

26

ONCE AGAIN WE
SAY GOODBYE

I WAS PACKING MY DUFFEL BAG, GETTING READY for my trip to Fort Benning, GA. My brothers, Danny and Dave, came into my room.

"You're leaving already?"

"I am."

"You can't leave, we never had a game of catch."

I said, "You know, you're right. Get the mitts and the ball."

Before I had left for the service my younger brothers and I would play catch or run bases till it got dark out. I forgot how much I liked playing with my brothers and sisters. We were an active family, playing sports and building go-karts and mini bikes. I had forgotten how much fun they were. I had been caught up in my own little world and I had forgotten about their world. I quickly made amends and spent more time with them the last two days I was at home. I took them for hot dogs and Cokes, milkshakes, and to the movies. I made peace with my brothers and sisters and made them understand they were still a large part of my life.

My dad and mom had a better understanding of what I had gone through. My dad already knew all of this. During World War II he was at the Battle of the Bulge and helped push the Germans back across the Ardennes into Germany. It was the last battle of World War II in Europe.

I really had to rediscover the most important thing in life, and that was family. While gone for a year in a war zone I had been deprived of my family. You have your close buddies who are working side by side with you; these buddies are your family. It's kind of strange. When I left Vietnam I felt a little guilty leaving them to fight a war without me. I guess that's the reason so many guys went back. It certainly wasn't the money.

The morning I left I finished packing and put on my class As and my dad drove me to O'Hare Airport. This time it was different; I was going down south to Georgia, not to a foreign country. I was not going to be in danger. But he never liked it when I was flying on those "contraptions," as he called them. He couldn't figure how they flew or the noise they made. He pulled up to the United terminal and we both got out and said our goodbyes. Once again there was an awkward moment of silence as our eyes welled up with tears.

I managed to blubber something like, "I'll be home for Christmas."

All he could say was, "Yeah, Christmas." I smiled and walked away. I was swallowed up in the crowd. But when you're six-foot-seven, people see you for a long time, even in a crowd.

Before I got to the ticket counter I was approached by a couple of Hare Krishnas looking for donations to their cause. I politely declined and started to walk away.

As I walked away, one of them sneered at me and said, "Did you kill any babies today?"

I stopped dead in my tracks and turned and walked back to him and his partner and said, "No I haven't, but the day is still young." I threw my duffel bag at the one Hare Krishna and grabbed the other one who was doing all the talking. I said, "Do you really want to start something right now?" We stared each other down for so long it seemed like an eternity. Security came and separated us and I went on my way. I was grinning. I thought to myself, *This is going to be a reoccurring situation as long as the war is going on.*

I picked up my duffel bag and casually walked to the ticket counter and purchased a military standby ticket to Atlanta with a connection to Columbus, GA. The flight to Atlanta was uneventful, and the flight to Columbus was short and arrived on time.

I caught a shuttle bus to Ft. Benning and signed in to my new company, which happened to be another Chinook company. It was called the 205th Aviation Company. As I was signing into the company I noticed a burlap bag sitting on the chair next to me. Then I noticed the bag moving around and I heard hissing noises coming from the bag. I asked the company clerk what was hissing in the bag.

He looked at me as he pulled the snake out of the bag and said, "It's just my pet boa constrictor, Harmon."

I froze for a moment while I regained my composure and then said to him, "Are you fucking crazy?"

He gave me a quizzical look and said, "He's harmless." Just then the executive officer came in and saw what was happening. He ordered him to put the snake back in the bag and put the bag in his car. The clerk protested that the snake would die.

The exec said, "Good." I agreed with the officer.

I finished signing in and was directed upstairs to the barracks. These barracks had been built in the sixties. There were two men to a room. Down the hall were toilets and shower facilities. The company headquarters was on the first floor and the mess hall was at the end of the building. You didn't have to go far for your meals.

I introduced myself to my new roommate and I could tell we were going to get along. Morning formation was at eight o'clock. This was where all the information was conveyed to you and attendance taken. In all the Army movies you watch, you see four ranks of men standing at attention and then at ease.

This is when all the snide remarks and grab-assing happens. It's better to be in the last row of the formation because you are relatively safe from any mischief.

Not only do they convey information to you during formation, but they also inspect your uniform and your appearance. You have to make sure to clean your uniform, shine your boots, and be clean shaven with a decent haircut.

My Platoon Sergeant would tell us only once to get a haircut. If you didn't, it was an Article 15 of the Uniform Code of Justice, which meant they took twenty-five dollars from you till you got the haircut or shaved. This was going to be my life in the Army in the United States. We called this the "Brown Boot Army." Oh yes, I almost forgot—they would inspect your room to see if the beds were made and the floor was cleaned and waxed. *This is bullshit*, I thought. *I could put a stop to all this crap if I went back to Vietnam.*

I think that's what they wanted you to do. I was reasonably sure I was not going back to Vietnam, so I had to get good at standing inspection and keeping my room clean. I didn't have a hooch maid here to pick up after me and clean my uniforms.

27

GOOD OL'
SOUTHERN HOSPITALITY?

A FTER MORNING FORMATION IT WAS TIME TO go to work down at the flight line. In Vietnam I was on flight status as a flight engineer on my own Chinook. Here I was on a maintenance team servicing and repairing other people's Chinooks. I was not happy about the situation. I requested to be put on flight status and was told they had too many E-6s and flight engineer was an E-6 slot; maybe they would find a crew chief slot for me in time. I had to bide my time and not sulk about it and be more professional about it.

Life at Ft. Benning wasn't too bad. I met a lot of guys I had gone to Chinook school with at Ft. Eustis, VA. In fact it was like old home week. I settled into military life and started playing flag football and volleyball for the 205th Aviation Co.

The Army liked it if you participated in sports and played for the company team. I was actually having a good time. One day I met a couple of other guys who were leaving the post on a Saturday afternoon. They were carrying golf clubs.

I said, "Where are you going?"

They said, "To the golf course."

"Can I go?" They said I could, but that I had to rent clubs at the course. I told them I had never played before.

They said, "That's ok, you can learn." They taught me well and I shot 115. I was hooked from that day on. To this day I still play golf. My new friends and I moved into a house on a cul-de-sac. It had three bedrooms, with a large backyard. The house was furnished and ready to go.

The Army gave me a BAQ (Bachelor's Allowance Quarters) allowance to help pay for the house. I was supposed to maintain my room on the fort, but new soldiers were coming back from Vietnam every day and they needed my room. So actually, it was just like an eight to four-thirty job. Every day we would get up and drive into the fort, have breakfast, go to formation, and then go to the flight line and work. After work we would go to dinner, and then go to football practice. After practice we would go to our house.

Our main pastime was trying to meet and date Southern women. This was a daunting, difficult task; we were not too popular because they knew we weren't going to stay for long. They knew we were G.I.s because of our short hair. We kept trying to grow our hair long but to no avail. I was constantly being told to get my hair cut. I'd worn my hair longer in Vietnam. Some guys resorted to wearing wigs on the weekends. I thought this was the most ridiculous thing I had ever seen. Did they think that these women were stupid or something? If anyone can tell whether someone is wearing a wig, it's a woman.

The people in military towns didn't like us, but they liked our money. I thought to myself, *What ever happened to good old Southern hospitality?* Wouldn't you know it, they were still fighting the Civil War down there. I was only spending eighteen months there, though, so I could live with it.

We made our rounds to all the nightclubs and titty bars. It got so we knew the first name of every dancer in Columbus, GA, and what size her breasts were. We heard of a strip club ten miles outside of town that was supposed to be fantastic; the women were goddesses walking around half naked all the time. It really sounded too good to be true.

We took my friend's 1949 Chevy sedan that we called "The Queen." This car had a mind of its own. She would start up fine when it was cold, but after you ran her for a while, shut her off, and went to restart her, she wouldn't go.

We pulled up in front of a ramshackle old building that looked like it was going to fall down any second. We checked out the address again and sure enough, it was the place. We could hear music from inside and the parking lot was jammed. We walked into the place but we weren't ready for what we saw. We were ushered to a table near the stage. On stage was a large, fat girl dancing her heart out. The waitress came over wearing only a vest. Her breasts were hanging out, and, oh yes, she had one front tooth missing. We thought it was amateur night for fat girls or hefty farm girls. We ordered four beers. We thought about leaving, but we knew that damn 1949 Chevy wasn't going to start.

The waitress came back with our beers and she asked if we wanted to run a tab. We paid the bill right away. Just then the fat girl on stage was working up a sweat and she started flinging those artillery shells for breasts around. The sweat was flying off her into our beers. We drank them anyway. The next time we were ready when she let go with the sweat. We covered our glasses.

This was probably the lowest time of my life at Ft. Benning. It was a bizarre place. I asked the waitress when the skinny girls danced.

She looked at me kind of weird and she said, "She's up there now. Wait till you see the next one." As the next one came out, we took one look and kept our hands over our beers. I thought to myself, *Can this night get any worse?*

Here we were, stuck at a back country roadhouse with a bunch of overweight, naked women. All because the fucking Queen would not start. Well, the night got worse because our waitress, the half-naked, chunky girl with the tooth missing, took a shine to me. She kept giving me free beers. Don't think my buddies didn't notice this. She would come over and stroke the back of my neck and smile. I chose to ignore these subtle hints. I was trying to be polite as possible, but she would have none of that. My buddies were of no help in rescuing me.

Finally she came over, sat on my knee, and told me her boyfriend was working all night at the grain elevator and would I like to fill in for him tonight? Before my buddies could respond, I politely told her I had duty in the morning and I was flying out to a different fort.

She looked at me and said, "Oh my god, you're a flyboy?"

I said "Yes, and I'll be back next week." What I should have said was, "I don't date women who outweigh me." But I didn't because she was sincere and we were in a strange place. My knee was starting to feel the effects of a large woman sitting on it. It was crying out in pain. Thank god the manager came over and told her she had more customers to wait on. She got up off of my knee and told me she would be back. She disappeared into the crowd and we left.

I limped out of the place past the bouncer. He yelled at us, "Y'all come back now, ya hear?" We got to The Queen and waved our hands over the hood and asked the car gods to start that miserable Chevy. We piled into her and crossed our fingers. When my buddy put the key in and turned, the starter slowly turned over, groaning the whole time. Finally she started and we breathed a sigh of relief and thanked the car gods.

We drove on down the road, not paying attention to the road signs. We discovered we had got sidetracked a little and had to go through the town of Waverly Square. It was one o'clock in the morning as we drove through the sleepy little town. It was a quaint little village just like you see on postcards. Even at night I could see the beauty of this place, a little town that time had forgotten and crime had not discovered yet. I liked it.

We drove past the town square and noticed the municipal buildings and small shops. The all-night café had a light on and we noticed a deputy sheriff drinking coffee at the lunch counter. He looked up and spied us slowly driving by. We got on the main road leading to the highway, picked up our speed, and thought we were out of the woods. A bright light was behind us and I looked in the side mirror and got that sick feeling you get when you see the Mars lights on a police cruiser. "Fuck," "shit," "goddamn," were the words used to curse our luck that night.

We pulled over and got out our military IDs and waited for the deputy to approach the car. He came to the back of the car and told us to get out of the car. He ordered the driver to open the trunk and stand back. We all watched him start tapping the sides of the trunk and pulling back the carpet.

He looked at us and asked, "Do you know why I stopped you?" We assumed it was for speeding or something like that. "No. I pulled you over for suspicion of running moonshine." We snickered a little. We thought this was a big joke, but it wasn't to him. We assured him we were soldiers stationed at Ft. Benning.

The black Chevy we were driving was an excellent car for transporting moonshine. It was low in the back and had a large trunk space. Once again we assured him we were not moonshiners. He rubbed his chin like he was thinking it over.

Then he said, "If you're not moonshiners, why haven't you shut off your car?" Apparently, runners never shut off their cars.

We told him we hadn't shut it off because it wouldn't start up again and that we'd have to wait two hours before it would. The deputy looked at us and said, "Yeah, my cousin Merle had a Chevy just like this and he had to carry a water hose around with him in the trunk. The starter would get too hot and then he hooked up the water hose and hosed down the starter to cool it off. The car was a pain in the ass." He looked at us and said, "You boys just made the mistake of driving this car in a dry county. I suggest you get in your car and take a left at the main highway and don't come back to this county with this car." We thanked him for not arresting us and got into The Queen and slowly drove away.

We had to drop off two guys at the barracks and then we could go home. We approached the gate at Ft. Benning and the MP waved us through. We drove to the 205th Aviation Company area and saw the oddest thing. The whole company was milling around in their underwear. One hundred guys standing around in their underwear waiting for something.

I said, "Let's see what's going on." I walked up to one of the guys and I asked, "What's going on?"

He said, "Tommy, that motherfucking company clerk, lost that motherfucking snake somewhere in the barracks. That snake was a nine foot boa constrictor."

I started laughing out loud. All these guys were tough, brazen Vietnam veterans. They were gunners, crew chiefs, and flight engineers. And they all looked pretty funny standing around in their underwear. At about three in the morning they finally found that snake. In Vietnam we would have shot it. Jonesy, the company clerk, came out of the building with the snake wrapped around his body. All of a sudden everyone was quiet; no insults and no more threats. The snake was taken to a local zoo and never heard from again.

28

BACK ON FLIGHT STATUS

I TOILED FOR THREE MONTHS ON A MAINTENANCE TEAM and one day my efforts paid off. I was called into the Old Man's office and told to get a flight physical first thing in the morning. I was back on flight status, which is where I wanted to be. The next morning I got a flight physical and passed with flying colors, even the vision test which I was a little worried about; fortunately it was 20/20. I was not going to be the flight engineer because in the States I would have to be an E-6 and I was an E-5. I was going to be the crew chief. That was all right with me. At least I was back flying, where I belonged.

The missions weren't dangerous like in Vietnam. In fact, they were a little mundane and boring, but at least I wasn't getting shot at. Fort Benning is the home of the jump school for all the paratroopers in the United States. Students from all branches of the services would come to Ft. Benning to learn how to be a paratrooper. Being a crew chief on a Chinook once again was a good duty for me; it was a chance to participate in the training. I was getting flight pay and my normal E-5 pay, but not hazardous duty pay like I had received in Vietnam.

Life was pretty good for me now, but thoughts of reenlisting were creeping back into my head and I was seriously considering it. I never told anyone because they would think me crazy. If the Army had offered me flight school I think I would have jumped at the opportunity. My time was filled up from morning till night. In the morning I was flying training missions as a crew chief and in the late afternoon I was playing football for the 205th Aviation. My days and nights were pretty filled, but on the weekends I had plenty of time to get into trouble.

The days were whizzing by and I had almost forgotten about the medal I was to receive. One day the First Sergeant called me into his office and reminded me about the medal presentation. I was to be decorated by General Orwin C. Talbot, the Commandant of Ft. Benning. I was to have my class A uniform cleaned and pressed. All my decorations should be mounted on my uniform. My dress shoes were to be spit polished, my hair cut to military levels, and my face clean shaven. My parents were notified and asked to attend. One week before the ceremony I was once again summoned to the First Sergeant's office. *That's twice in one week!*, I thought.

The First Sergeant is the highest ranked enlisted man in the company; it's his responsibility to run the company and the company commander signs whatever the First Sergeant puts in front of him. The First Sergeant is usually called "Top," meaning Top Sergeant, and this rank is an E-8. I checked in with the company clerk and he showed me into the First Sergeant's office.

I said, "Hey, Top, you sent for me?"

He looked at me and asked me, "What is this shit, you're not re-upping?"

"It's not shit, Top, I'm not." He looked at me in disgust and told me to sit down. I started thinking this guy had a burr in his saddle. *What's with these military guys, they just won't give up? They are worse than Jehovah's Witnesses on a Sunday afternoon!* He abruptly got off the subject of my reenlisting and got to the matter at hand.

"You have been chosen to crew on a Chinook from this company carrying the president and his family's baggage from Homestead Air Force Base to Key Biscayne, Florida. This duty is on the weekends and you'll get extra pay and housing allowance. The only drawback is, you have to pass a top security clearance. Can you pass this clearance?"

I was a little stunned. I said, "Let me get this straight—you want me to crew on a Chinook picking up the president's baggage and bringing it to Key Biscayne, Florida, and back to Homestead Air Force Base?"

"That's right, but you have to pass the security clearance first."

I accepted the duty; I thought it would be pretty cool. They sequestered me in a barracks room until the security check was finished and then I was let out for normal duty. They sent out Secret Service agents to the neighborhood where I had lived in Chicago and questioned all my neighbors, friends, and relatives. Everything checked out OK and I was given a top secret security clearance because I had access to the president's baggage. I thought this to be an even better duty and evidently the First Sergeant thought I would re-up. Boy was he wrong.

29

NIXON, AGNEW, AND TRICIA

I WAS ACCEPTED INTO THE NEW DUTY AND I was to start the following weekend. All my flight uniforms were new and my boots were spit-shined. My personal appearance was OK because I had thought I was going to receive the DFC the following week, but they pushed it back a month because of the special duty I was now on.

I was given instructions on how to act when in the presence of dignitaries. Do this, don't do that—basically, keep my mouth shut and speak only when spoken to. I actually thought this was not going to be a problem for me because I was in awe of everything and everybody that I came into contact with during this duty.

I had Secret Service men riding on the aircraft with me. The flight crews stayed at a hotel near Homestead Air Force Base and on the beach. When it came time, we would go back to Key Biscayne and pick up the First Family's luggage and fly back to Homestead. The president and family would fly on *Army One* or

Army Two. This is when I would catch a glimpse of Nixon or his wife Pat. She was very nice to the flight crews; she would offer us lemonade or iced tea. I was really starting to like this duty.

The Secret Service men who did the background check on me had scoured my old neighborhood looking for any unfavorable information about me. My neighbors stood by me and gave the agents the standard answer, which was, "He's such a nice boy, what has he done?" The agents did tell them I would be working in a government capacity. When the agents left, the neighbors all ran over to my parents' house wanting to know what was going on. My parents knew nothing and were busy trying to get ahold of me. I couldn't tell them very much at first. When the truth came out, their chests were sticking out so far it was like they had received a medal. But that's OK, they were just proud. I just had to keep my smart mouth shut—and this was a daily problem.

In the late spring we were bringing in a large load of luggage for the First Family and the Secret Service agents. We landed on the helipad on the Key Biscayne compound and we shut down the aircraft to be unloaded. I lowered the ramp and undid the straps that secured the luggage. I was waiting for the house boys to come out and unload the aircraft.

Instead, a tall, lanky young man came out to the ship and told me that Tricia needed her makeup bag. I quickly, and without thinking, told him that Tricia didn't need a makeup bag, she was much too pretty. I found the bag, a little suitcase with a mirror and about eight pounds of makeup. I handed it to the young man who walked like he had a two-by-four wedged up his ass. I thought that was the end of it.

Later on, I was summoned to a small office on the compound in front of a full bird colonel. I thought to myself, *Wow, somebody's in trouble.* I soon found out the somebody was me.

As it turned out, the young man who had asked for the makeup bag was going to marry Tricia Nixon in three months. This full bird colonel laid into me, and when he got tired a major took a turn at telling me what they thought of me. Everyone in the room was upset except me and I was starting to get there myself. I couldn't figure out what I had done wrong. These guys were really making a living chewing my ass out.

Finally they stopped yelling and asked me, "Well, what have you got to say for yourself?"

I decided to smooth the situation over and say something real formal and military. I came to attention and spoke clearly and loudly and said, "Sir, my sword is yours and the First Family's and it won't happen again." There was a moment of silence while the officers in the room looked at each other and then back to me.

The colonel spoke slowly. "Son, your record got you here. Now you have to change and adapt to an Army in the United States." He dismissed me and I saluted and he returned it and I breathed a sigh of relief. I was wondering if that line would work anywhere; but no, just in the Army. In Vietnam you can get away with a lot of things, but not in the States.

****

One of the coolest guys I met on this duty was Vice President Spiro Agnew. He was a very gregarious man who enjoyed meeting and talking with the flight crews. He would come over and shake our hands and ask how we were. I thought he was going to be the next President of the United States. But sadly, two years later he was forced to resign his office because of funds misspent on a campaign back in his home state of Maryland. The closer I got to the politicians, the more I got the feeling that what I was really looking at were future convicts. The Nixon administration was riddled with them. I used to take a lot of crap from people because

I served under Nixon and Agnew. The truth is, we serve the office, not the man or woman. You may not like the dignitaries whom you serve, but it's the office they hold that you have to respect. I think these people get into politics to change the world and to make it a better place to live. Then something happens and they get seduced by the power and the many people who are serving them.

I really liked this duty and I got very good at it. It gave me a false sense that my star was rising and the sky was the limit. Unfortunately, it wasn't. You hang around these people long enough, you might start thinking like them; not good. I don't know if I wanted to be like these people. I was under the impression that people went into public office to help their fellow man and to try to make the country a better place to live, to pass laws, and make things right for all the people who have been wronged in this country. But really, the people we have elected see this country as one big apple pie and they want their share. There is nothing great about these people; I should know, because I did serve with great people. We served for a common goal and we performed brilliantly. I can't say that about the Nixon administration. They needed to lose an election and to be humbled before the American people and the Americans who were serving and fighting in foreign wars.

To be fair, there are people who do care about the American people and they are trying to do the job they were elected to, but they seem to be in a minority. This was one path I wasn't going to go down. I was going to do my one year and be done with it.

30

ALL THAT BRASS

THE ARMY FINALLY DECIDED TO DECORATE ME ON March 17th, 1972. I had ten days' notice to get my parents to come down to Ft. Benning. They drove all the way down from Chicago. My mother loved the pomp and regiment of an Army fort. When they approached the main gate they were stopped by the MPs. One of them questioned my parents about where they were going and who they were going to see and what their business was. My mother told them they were coming to see their son, who was to be decorated with the Distinguished Flying Cross.

"Maybe you've heard of him." she said, "He's in helicopters. He's in the 205th Aviation Co."

The MP replied, "That would be near the airfield."

Then my mother couldn't resist asking him about his white gloves. "Where did you get your beautiful white gloves?" The MP was cool and courteous, and responded to all their questions and showed them the route to take to the 205th Aviation Company area.

All fort activities are run by a bugle call. You wake up to a bugle and you go to sleep to a bugle. As my parents were driving to the company area, they heard a bugle and everyone got out of their cars and stood at attention. The bugle call was retreat, which means end of working day. So, my parents got out of the car in the middle of the road and stood at attention. They were thrilled. The pomp and circumstance of military life.

They were escorted to the airfield, and once there they asked where I was. Once again they were escorted to the flight line, where all the helicopters were parked. They walked the entire distance from the maintenance building to the last parking spot, where I was. They walked up the ramp of the Chinook and were mesmerized by the whole experience. I was making entries into the log book and looked up at them and smiled. They had no idea what they were looking at and had so many questions. I answered their questions as best as I could. My dad was enamored with the complexity of the Chinook; it just blew him away.

He kept asking me, "Do you understand all these mechanical gadgets and what each one does and how it operates?"

I said, "Yeah, Dad, I understand everything about this aircraft, otherwise they wouldn't let me fly on it." I took him up top and showed him the engines and transmissions and he was impressed.

He said, "It's amazing this thing gets off the ground."

"Dad, at one time this was the most powerful helicopter in the free world. It's going to be around a long time." My dad was a truck mechanic by trade. He had learned his trade in the Army during World War II. He was the last truck in the convoys that were feeding General Patton's Third Army during his campaign in Europe. Any trucks that would break down, my dad was there to repair them and get them back with the convoy. When the Battle of the Bulge broke out, he was transferred to an artillery unit. The unit he was in helped the Allies push the Nazis back across the border into Germany. After the war, he worked for trucking companies as a mechanic and made a good living and managed to raise nine kids. That, to me, was quite a feat. I would never want to do that.

He was very good at what he did but somehow technology had passed him by. When he looked at the Chinook, to him it looked like a mess of wires and hydraulics and transmissions.

Can a great man be a mechanic and a father of nine and go off to war at age nineteen and be part of the Greatest Generation? To me he can, and will always be a great man.

My mom was still talking about the MP's white gloves and how straight and formal he was. She liked the military traditions that were carried out during the day; everyone marching in formation, the raising and lowering of the flag, the bugle system that notified everyone what to do. She took one look at the Chinook and decided it was much too complicated and she referred to it as a large calliope. I explained the inner workings of the Chinook to them and I might as well have been speaking in Latin. They just nodded their heads in agreement, not knowing what they were agreeing to. They were in awe of this large beast of a helicopter. Sometimes I felt that way myself.

I started closing up the ship and tying down the blades and my mother said, "When is supper around here?"

I said, "In the next hour."

She said, "Good, we want to eat in the mess hall with the rest of the troops."

I said, "Why would you want to do that?"

She replied, "We want to show our support for the troops." I looked at my dad and he rolled his eyes from side to side and then he looked up.

He looked at her and asked her, "What's next, Dorothy, would you like to try out the latrines in support of the troops?" She did not get her way, which was fine with me. We decided to dine at one of Columbus, GA's finer restaurants.

The next morning I was to be decorated. I was a little nervous as the day started. I picked up my class As from the dry cleaner. I spit-shined my dress shoes for two hours, until I could see my reflection in them. I polished my brass and arranged my combat ribbons. The suit was a perfect fit. The little Chinese tailor had done an excellent job of fitting me. The suit was so perfect, I did it an injustice by putting it on. I looked great. It fit so well it made me put my shoulders back, my chest out, and my stomach in.

My parents picked me up and drove me to the auditorium. They went into the audience and I was ushered backstage. On the way back I spent my time saluting lieutenants, captains, majors, colonels, and yes, one or two generals. They explained the procedure to me and asked me if I understood. I never saw so much brass in all my time in the Army. Dumbfounded, I shook my head "yes."

I walked over to a corner and lit up a cigarette and thought about *that* day. I was running scenes in my mind about what had gone wrong. I kept thinking that we were the last Chinook to get in at that firebase. We were shot up going in and shot up going out. So much had gone wrong *that* day, it's hard to believe we got out with sixty ARVN soldiers. In my head I was doing a rerun of the mission. Little did I know that this rerun would play for the rest of my life, sometimes at the most inopportune times.

Somebody came over to me and touched my arm and said, "Specialist Messenger, you're on." I walked onto the stage with the other soldiers who were getting decorated that day and I felt proud to be in good company. They put a temporary hanger below my ribbon bar so General Talbot could just hang the medal on the hanger. You wouldn't want him trying to pin it on you. Chances are he would spill more blood than was necessary. Can you imagine, losing more blood getting the medal than earning the medal?

General Orwin C. Talbot was a kindly looking man who could have passed for somebody's grandfather. He moved down the ranks, decorating and engaging in conversation with the other recipients, and by the time he got down to me and placed the medal on me, I gave him that dirty grin that I was famous for and I saluted smartly. He smiled back at me with his own dirty grin and returned the salute. I knew then we were cut from the same cloth and we were both rogues.

After the ceremony my parents came up to me and congratulated me. I looked at my dad and he was beaming. To my surprise, General Talbot came over to me and called me by my first name. He said he had read the combat action reports and was impressed at how we had performed *that* day. I told him that everything had gone wrong and we had to improvise what to do.

He understood what had gone wrong and he said, "We, as officers, plan the missions, but things do go wrong; that's why we rely on our NCOs to make the plans work. This medal is acknowledgment of your ability that day to make things right and complete the mission. Forget about all that Hollywood crap you see in the movies. It's just crap! Nothing is easy in combat. You have to have the ability to think while under stress. You thought your way through the stress of combat and completed your mission." I thanked him and once again shook his hand and wished him well.

My parents went to pick up the car, which gave me time to think about the last year and how it was going to affect my future and what my future was. I had time to think about all the men who had received this medal before me. I think my biggest concern was not to dishonor this medal or myself because of the men who wore it before me and the men who had died earning it. As I walked out of the building I realized I had two or three paths to pick from. *Once again I'm at the crossroads. Wonder where I'm going?*

31

FINAL THOUGHTS

F LASH AHEAD FORTY-TWO YEARS. IT'S NOW 2013. Every day I pass by this medal, because it hangs in a shadow box in my bedroom. It's not for everyone to see, just me. It's a constant reminder to maintain good moral character. I think I have done a pretty good job of doing just that, although it has been close a couple of times.

There have been six military actions since I left Vietnam: Nicaragua, Grenada, Kosovo, Desert Storm, The Afghanistan War, and the second Iraq War. In the last twenty years there have been too many wars. I think our best and brightest are being sacrificed for wars that mean nothing. I believe the guard dogs are sick and it's going to get worse. The guard dogs represent the military and the lambs are the people of the United States. With so many wars in the last twenty years the guard dogs haven't had a chance to heal. It is up to the lambs to heal the guard dogs of their sicknesses, bind their wounds, replace their limbs, and treat their mental problems.

The VA hospitals are overflowing right now and it's getting worse. So I say to all you lambs: don't scream and holler about the money it's costing you. Your life has gone on as if nothing has happened. Take out your checkbook, pay your taxes, and do it cheerfully, not begrudgingly. Then take a walk through a VA hospital and see what the price of war is. I could tell you, but you should see it for yourself.

Before World War II the United States was not a world power. After the war, it assumed its place as a world power and has held that title for the last sixty-two years. In my opinion, in order for the United States to remain a world power, we must always support and defend our own Constitution, so the world can see that we live by and enforce it. Whenever we invade and conquer another nation we must not occupy that nation very long. We must rebuild it, provide aid, and then we must withdraw in a timely manner. We should always show compassion and sorrow whenever it is called for and always demonstrate diplomacy and stay open all lines of communication.

I think President Teddy Roosevelt said it best: We must walk softly and carry a big stick. Meaning, we must be diplomatic with our enemies, but if that doesn't work, use our military might when appropriate. Many foreign nations have made the mistake of thinking that the United States has no stomach for war. Who the fuck are they kidding? Don't they go to our nation's capital and see all the war memorials? When we can't find somebody to fight, we fight each other.

This weekend I'm in Washington, D.C. for the 179th and 180th Aviation reunions. I haven't seen some of these guys for forty-two years. I am surrounded by great men who served in Vietnam and have gone on to make a life for themselves here at home. We look at old photo albums of us when we were nineteen, twenty years old. The kidding and the cajoling start as if we never left

Vietnam. Some of us have hair; some of us don't. Most of us have gained weight.

The plan was to go to the Vietnam Veterans Memorial Wall and the National World War II Memorial and pay our respects. As luck would have it, the government closed down all monuments and museums because Congress did not raise the debt ceiling. We sat at dinner and discussed the problems that Congress created, and we decided to go anyway and force our way into the closed off areas if necessary. After forty-four years, a bunch of sixty-something Vietnam vets were going to storm the barricades at the Vietnam Memorial. Fortunately, we walked right through the barricades without any problems. Thank God.

We walked along the Wall, stopping to look at the names of soldiers we had served with. We wept and prayed. Memories of missions and the men I served with played in my head as if I had gone back in time and were there. I was sorry that the men on the Wall didn't come back. But I did. It was very emotional, thinking about the sacrifices the people of this nation make to maintain the freedoms we have and hold so dear.

As you might have guessed, I have become one of the guys on the train at the beginning of the story. I now have the wife, the kids, the mortgage, and the bills, bills, and more bills. Sometimes when people ask me what I do, I want to say I'm a flight engineer, on a CH-47 Chinook for the 179th Aviation Company. That's the cool answer.

Acknowledgments

A NYBODY WHO KNOWS ME WOULD PROBABLY tell you they were surprised I wrote a book, and I would halfheartedly agree with them. Lisa Wallace saw it differently. She was my counselor at the V.A. and as part of treatment for PTSD she asked me to journal my time in Vietnam. This I could not do. What I could do was remember stories that happened while I was there. As I wrote, my wife Barbara read the stories and edited them. Later, her sister Linda joined her in the process. When I finished writing I was perfectly willing to put the big alligator clip on the manuscript and throw it onto a closet shelf and close the door. Lisa, Barbara and Linda had other ideas.

My wife encouraged me to continue writing. Linda S.Wold, Ed.D. taught me how to take constructive criticism and modify my style to make it flow better. My niece, Becky Straple, a Ph.D. candidate at Western Michigan University, edited my story twice. She assured me that a lay person who has never been in the military should be able to read and understand this story. My Vietnam buddies Byron Raney, Gene Womack, Robert Vickery, Steve Richter, and Stan Neckermann contributed photos and supported me just like they did forty-three years ago. I am humbly grateful to all who have mentored me during this journey.

About the Author

T OM MESSENGER WAS BORN AND RAISED in Chicago, Illinois.
He is the recipient of the Distinguished Flying Cross, the Air
Medal, and the Vietnamese Cross of Gallantry. He suffers from Post-
Traumatic Stress Disorder, which led to the creation of this book.
When he couldn't sleep, he wrote. He presently lives with his wife
in Oswego, Illinois.

CPSIA information can be obtained at www.ICGtesting.com
Printed in the USA
BVOW09s0747301014

372794BV00011B/436/P

9 781555 718060